BRITAIN'S EVERYDAY HEROES

To the millions of everyday heroes throughout Britain,
with thanks for all that you do

BRITAIN'S EVERYDAY HEROES

THE MAKING OF THE GOOD SOCIETY

GORDON BROWN

WITH

MAINSTREAM
PUBLISHING

EDINBURGH AND LONDON

First published in Great Britain in 2007 by
MAINSTREAM PUBLISHING COMPANY
(EDINBURGH) LTD
7 Albany Street
Edinburgh EH1 3UG

ISBN 9781845963071

A catalogue record for this book is available
from the British Library

Typeset in Helvetica and Sabon

Printed in Great Britain by
Clays Ltd, St Ives plc

FSC
Mixed Sources
Product group from well-managed
forests and other controlled sources

Cert no. SGS - COC - 2061
www.fsc.org
© 1996 Forest Stewardship Council

CONTENTS

Pathfinders

AUTHOR'S NOTE

None of the people in this book would describe themselves as heroes. None seek personal acclaim or lavish remuneration for their work. Most would, I suspect, identify more comfortably with Archbishop Romero's aspiration 'not to have more, but to be more'.

Each one has inspired with their passion, their determination and their triumphs. And while there are details of their life stories far outside the scope of this book, I know that many of them have overcome personal tragedies and challenges to do what they now do.

I am grateful to the leaders of Community Links, led by David Robinson and Richard McKeever, who have researched the stories that are now told. And I am grateful to them and to Gila Sacks and John Newbiggin for introducing me to some of the people doing so much for our country.

I know that these men and women who are achieving so much are not alone. Day after day, throughout the UK, others like them are quietly changing lives, building together the good society. They are, for me, Britain's everyday heroes.

I have written this book to acknowledge the work of these men and women and millions like them who do so much for our country and are often unrecognised. They represent the best of Britain and should make us optimistic about our national future.

INTRODUCTION

A PERSONAL JOURNEY

T his book is about a journey round Britain, but it is not a
travelogue or an account of times and places. This book
is about people in all parts of Britain who have given me a
fresh insight into the needs and aspirations of our country,
what is great about it now and how it can become greater in
the future.

I have had the privilege of meeting the unassuming woman
who has been the inspiration behind community reconciliation
in Northern Ireland, and I have been introduced by friends
at Community Links to the leader of a community campaign
tackling gang culture in Manchester. I visited a housing estate
in Leicester in the East Midlands and there met the woman
who has endured personal attacks and gone on to be a
leader in its transformation. I have talked to the founder of
an intergenerational arts project strengthening community
cohesion in London and met the dedicated child psychologist
who set out to end illiteracy in one of the most deprived areas
of Scotland.

This book also tells the story of the parish councillor
committed to the regeneration of his Warwickshire village and
passionate about encouraging young people to participate in
the running of local services. It is about the campaigner who
has established the world's first Fairtrade Town and the founder
of the mySociety project who is transforming the way we use

the Internet as a tool of democracy and active citizenship. And it is about the work of the creative pioneers who brought the arts to a deprived housing estate, gardening to refugees and opera to the homeless.

These are also the stories of public servants and community leaders reaching far beyond the confines of their official remits to give their time and energy to meet the real needs they witness first hand; of a new generation of social entrepreneurs, people who have proved that successful business can indeed benefit their communities; and of men and women offering one-to-one support, like the young man who chose to go back to help the law centre that once helped him to turn his life around and the athletics coach in his eighties who has inspired generation after generation of young people in his area.

In my travels, I have met men and women whom the spotlight of public attention usually neglects and visited places prosperity too often has passed by. So this is also the story of remaining pockets of poverty, deprivation and need that we must now tackle and of damage so often caused by drugs and by abuse. For across our country I have seen potential too often unfulfilled, talent too often wasted, the aspirations of the young too often unrealised.

But this book also tells of communities being transformed and revived, of good people who are mentoring the young, tackling antisocial behaviour and gun crime, addressing homelessness, environmental degradation and the alienation of young people. It is the story of dedicated men and women who are nurturing our young, encouraging our teenagers, caring for our disabled and empowering people who too often feel powerless and left out. And so these are accounts of personal achievement and victories against the odds that are truly inspirational. It teaches me that when a human hand reaches out for help, so often another hand reaches out to give that help. And I have come to understand what a fellow Scot from my home town, Kirkcaldy – the writer John Buchan – meant when he once said our task is not to put the greatness back into humanity but to elicit it, for the greatness is there already.

In the course of my travels, I have come to the view that weaknesses we see in Britain today can be overcome by our strengths; and it is because of the very greatest of all our strengths – the civic duty and resilience of the British people and their willing commitment to help their fellow citizens – that I believe so much in our country's future.

The first section of the book is the story of leaders who have sought to strengthen or to transform their own communities. They are the activists who have worked to enable those around them to believe in a better future. They are the pioneers developing new forms of community, new ways of belonging. They are the builders: the people who recognise that strong, cohesive, dynamic and caring communities are the best mechanisms for turning individual commitment into social change. They are essential to the building of the good society all of us wish for.

The second section tells of people devoting their time to individuals, nurturing the one-to-one relationships that are fundamental to tackling social challenges and to transforming lives. They are the carers whose patience and love is the backbone of families and communities across the country. They are the teachers and coaches nurturing young people's potential and enlarging their aspirations. They are the mentors building the essential human relationships that allow us to grow and learn, to build our confidence and our capabilities. They are the exemplifiers of the power of the human touch.

And the third section of this book tells the story of the pathfinders who are at the cutting edge of social change. They are the innovators developing new ways to use new ideas, technologies and resources to tackle new challenges. They are the entrepreneurs developing new models to apply the opportunities presented by business and enterprise to achieve social objectives. They are the creative minds taking risks and trying brand-new ways to solve problems and to help people. They are the guiding lights towards a new future for social action.

Of course I am aware of the great challenges we face today – from terrorism and security to environmental change – and the sense that the British way of life is under pressure. I am fully conscious of the fears and concerns each of us feels as we contemplate the future. But I am even more optimistic about Britain's future than I was a decade ago because in every part of the country I have seen good people striving to make Britain a better place. And everywhere I have travelled, I have been encouraged and inspired by meeting and listening to concerned citizens wanting to do more to make their neighbourhoods safe and strong, people who show a willing commitment to each other, day in and day out, year in and year out.

What I have seen convinces me that there is no problem so big in Britain that it cannot be fixed by what is already good in Britain, and that there is nothing so bad that may drag us down that cannot be addressed by what is good and can lift us all up: the energies of men and women inspired by the values that Britain first gave to the world – the timeless idea of civic duty and the responsibilities each of us accepts we owe to others. It is indeed the duties discharged by each of us that are the key to improving the well-being of us all.

So we need to celebrate the people who make the difference; recognise the growing spirit across Britain from social enterprise and corporate social responsibility to local community action and one-to-one mentoring that exemplifies what Beveridge called 'the driving power of social conscience'; and at the same time recognise how we can forge a new partnership between community organisations and government that should support them. Some people argue that government should just get out of the way and that the voluntary sector can be a cut-price replacement for government funding. But this attitude is not reflected in the views of the people I have met. Take Britain's six million carers. Our carers do not want government to walk away. Quite the opposite: carers want to know what government, working in partnership with them, can do to make their lives better – from respite care and financial backing to better training and pensions. And they want government to do more to empower them, as do voluntary organisations representing mothers looking for better childcare, young people's organisations calling for better youth services and elderly citizens calling for better services and new rights for the elderly. None of them see the voluntary sector as a cheaper alternative to what government should and must do to help. So this book is also the story of the partnership we need where each of us – government, voluntary sector and the individual – does what we can.

The values that matter for a good society – individuals doing their duty, communities coming together and a supportive government playing its part – are familiar to me. They were the values I grew up with in the industrial town of Kirkcaldy. Looking back on my youth, our lives revolved around not only the home but also the church, the youth club, the local football and rugby teams, the local tennis club, the Scouts and Boys' Brigades, and other organisations as varied as the Royal National Lifeboat Institution and the St John Ambulance and St Andrew's Societies, all of which were run by local people giving freely of their time.

Kirkcaldy then, like most towns, was enriched by a myriad of community organisations each supported by a network of voluntary effort: from the Red Cross and British Legion to St Vincent De Paul and all the churches and local faith groups. This was how it was in a local community: not in any sense a forced coming together; nor was it – as people sometimes portray community – some sentimental togetherness for the sake of appearances. People came together out of a largely unquestioned conviction that we help, support and care for each other and need each other, and can learn from each other and call on each other in times of difficulty. There was a sense that we owed obligations to each other because the people next door and in the next streets were indeed part also of what we all were; the idea of neighbourliness was woven into the way we led our lives.

Thinking back on it as I grew up and left the town, I realised that the whole community was really held together by men and women giving of their time voluntarily: as youth leaders and church elders, as football and sports coaches, as Scouts and Boys' Brigade helpers, as fundraisers for all the projects involved, as secretaries of local associations and clubs, as volunteers wherever there was need.

So while some people say you have only yourself or your family – and go on to conclude there is no such thing as society – I saw every day how individuals were encouraged and strengthened, made to feel they belonged, and in turn contributed as part of an intricate local network of trust, recognition and obligation that encompassed family, friends, school, church and dozens of local associations and voluntary organisations – often with local council and national government in support.

It is all too easy to romanticise about a Britain now gone or at risk of soon becoming the distant past and thus another country. Of course our world is now very different. Ours may be an era in which many of the traditional structures of society, association and voluntary engagement have declined. And of course participation in organised religion, in political parties, in trade unions, in uniformed groups has fallen in much of the country, as has participation in many formal structures and organisations traditionally built around the weekly or monthly meeting, the community centre or the church hall.

But there are now extraordinary new and exciting forms of civic life and social participation emerging even as we see the fading of older ways. The language of 'volunteering' no longer does justice to the range of new ways that people are finding to express their commitment to building a better society. Fewer of us may now choose to formally join a political party, but more of us than ever are participating in campaigns to effect change on the issues we care about by signing petitions, wearing a wristband, boycotting a product, lobbying Parliament. Traditional modes of association may have declined, but new associations from mother and toddler groups and sports clubs to organisations for the elderly have been formed, and modern technologies have opened up entirely new ways for us to communicate and to build new communities that support and mentor those in need, and pool our ideas and our knowledge for good. And alongside all the formal volunteering that continues to grow, we find the many, many informal networks of care and mutual support that are now flourishing across the country, bringing people together, connecting people and communities and offering help in whatever way it might be needed.

The world is changing fast, but, while it might manifest itself in very different ways today, that shared sense of common purpose I first experienced as a schoolboy still has the power to run deep in our villages, towns and cities across Britain. And it is not just an attachment to place or kith and kin who share the same history. It is also an attachment to shared values and ideals lived out daily across the country as people are connecting one-to-one, supporting each other and growing together.

A few months ago I finished a book about my heroes: the courageous people who inspired and still inspire me, whose strength of belief and character meant that, whatever the adversity, they kept going. Often we put our heroes on a pedestal, marvelling at their courage but never imagining we could emulate it. Courage, many people have said, is for the heroic, the celebrated and the elite. But I have met a great many ordinary people who have seen or experienced a need and who have responded to it in an extraordinary way, often going first, taking risks, braving disapproval and even ostracism and taking on entrenched interests. This is the courage being lived out every day in communities in every part of the country. Many of the individuals whose stories are told here would not see themselves as heroes, and all – modest as they are – have been anxious to stress the collaborative nature of their work and their achievements, but there is no doubt that they are all achieving something very special.

These men and women are people with beliefs and willpower; people who keep on doing what they think is right; people who choose not the easy option but the challenge and the difficulties that come with it. They are inspiring to me, but what is truly humbling and awe-inspiring is the realisation that the people I have been introduced to can be only a fraction – in all probability only a tiny fraction – of a far greater force for good. And if the deeds and achievements I saw and learnt about are representative – as I believe they are – then let us acknowledge gratefully the scale of what is being done and enlarge our sense of the possible and the vast potential of what might be achieved in the future.

The great American jurist Justice Warren once said that he read the newspaper sports pages first because their stories were of human achievements, and the front pages last because their stories were of human failings. If so much of the time we focus on what divides us, disturbs us or pulls us down, then this book is an attempt to focus afresh on what unites us, inspires us and lifts us up. I believe it is time to celebrate the best in Britain, and, by celebrating it and emulating it, build an even better future. So this is the story of everyday heroes: the kind of heroes who live next door, and in the next street, and throughout our neighbourhoods – the kind of heroes we might ourselves become. This is their story and the story of so many thousands more.

BUILDERS

The stories of people who spend their lives building and improving their neighbourhoods testify to the power of community as an essential force for social change in Britain today. In this section are the accounts of the people who are themselves building, rebuilding, strengthening and leading communities: the community campaigner working for reconciliation in Northern Ireland and the artist bringing together different cultures and generations in east London; the community activist in Leicester and parish councillor in Warwickshire, regenerating and reviving struggling communities; the Manchester mother working to turn around a community blighted by violence; and the people building entirely new types of community – the man who transformed Garstang into the world's first Fairtrade Town and the man who has built a unique community for homeless men and women in Cambridge.

These community builders are evidence, I believe, of a golden thread that runs through British history, is apparent throughout Britain today and is capable of renewing Britain in the future. This golden thread is the modern idea of civic society, arguably invented by Britain in the age of enlightenment. It is an idea rooted in what the Scottish philosopher Adam Fergusson called our 'civil responsibilities', eventually incorporating what Edmund Burke defined as 'little platoons': ideas we would recognise today as being at the heart of the voluntary sector and of community action.

This is my idea of Britain and Britishness today, with each member of society feeling connected to and playing a part in something bigger than themselves. Each of us – to paraphrase

Franklin Delano Roosevelt – doing what we can, with what we have, from where we are. In this vision of society, there is a sense of belonging that expands as we grow from family to friends and neighbourhood; a sense of belonging that ripples from places of learning and leisure and work and worship and eventually out beyond our home town and region to define us: in our nation, our time and our society.

Because there is such a thing as society: a community of communities, tens of thousands of local neighbourhood civic associations, unions, charities, voluntary organisations and volunteers, each one unique and each one very special. A Britain energised by a million centres of neighbourliness and compassion that together embody that very British idea: civic society.

This idea has deep roots in our history and our great social institutions: the churches, the mutual and friendly societies, the co-operative movement, the trade unions and all the legacies of the great Victorian philanthropists. In the nineteenth century, we led the world in the range, breadth and depth of our voluntary organisations and in the creation of a civic society. But in that age the contributions of ordinary people were perhaps overshadowed by the philanthropy of a few, and in our own age the efforts of this fertile voluntary sector came to be seen as insufficient in the face of the profound changes of the modern era. And so the public services provided by the state became the vehicle by which to guarantee the great freedoms that the pioneers could aspire to and argue for but never realise on their own: universal education, free healthcare for all, an old-age pension, child benefits, a welfare state.

In the last two centuries we have, as a society, thrown off the shackles of hierarchy and deference, and perhaps we have not yet fulfilled the promise of a more interdependent world: that we be joined together by the strongest possible bonds of community. But I am sure that if in the nineteenth century we relied on charities probably too much, and in the twentieth probably too little, in the twenty-first century voluntary and community action, often in partnership with publicly provided services, will be at the very heart of the way we govern ourselves. I see government empowering individuals and communities so that they are at the heart of decision-making and delivery. And I see community action going much further than traditional notions of giving or volunteering to encompass the active engagement of individuals and communities in all the myriad actions and commitments that drive social change. The importance of active engagement is described powerfully in the old Chinese proverb: 'Tell me and I forget, show me and I might remember, involve me and I understand', and it is in this way that the golden thread of civic society will be strengthened and renewed for new times. So this section suggests that community action will play a greater role than ever before in how we govern ourselves, provide for our needs and care for each other.

When the work of these community builders is replicated in each and every community, an energised civic society will become the inspiring and driving force it should be in twenty-first-century Britain.

1

ERINMA BELL

*If you want to see change, you must be part
of the change.*

One tragic event changed Erinma Bell's life and made her
the community leader she has become. When I met her
in Manchester, she told me how she and her husband and a
friend were returning from a work's Christmas night out when
they spotted a group of young people, and particularly one
threatening-looking man, lurking in an alleyway. 'I didn't like
the look of what I was seeing, but my husband told me I was
being paranoid. "I'm sure he has a gun," I said. "You're so
suspicious," he replied.

'But I was right enough: women's intuition you can call it.
For then I heard the shots: eleven or twelve times. I was right
behind my friend, and they just started shooting him. That's
when gun crime became a reality in my life. Before, it wasn't
part of my life, it was what I heard about on the news or what
I read in a newspaper. It didn't affect me close up. We were
saying it was happening in our community and we wanted
to make a difference, but you never really know what it's like
until it actually happens to you. I remember screaming, "No,
they're shooting, they're shooting him!" I ran over and started
shouting at them to stop. I dialled 999 while they finished
emptying their barrels. Then they just wandered off: they just
walked off and we had to deal with the aftermath. It was just
disgusting. I found it really, really disgusting that someone

could shoot another person in cold blood like that. When you experience it, it's shocking and it's awful.'

This experience left Erinma outraged but, as she explained, drove her not to despair but to a tireless search for answers. 'Nobody can tell me why those people shot my friend, but there were questions I felt could be answered, like how did they get hold of guns in the first place? Who's supplying the guns into our neighbourhood, because I know we don't have a gun factory in Moss Side. So that's why I got involved. I said, "We need to be asking the authorities questions like how these guns get into our neighbourhood. Questions like why it takes forty-five minutes for an ambulance to turn up." The answer community members gave me was, "That's how it is." I said, "What do you mean, that's how it is? It's not good enough."'

This shocking incident led Erinma to get involved in the community campaign against gang violence and eventually led her to form a group known as CARISMA – Community Alliance for Renewal Inner South Manchester Area – following several local shootings. She explained, 'CARISMA was set up when, after that series of shootings, a community demonstration, the Gang Stop march, was held. After the march, people felt really uplifted about having been heard, but then they wanted to do a bit more, to continue things, and I was the one saying we need to keep this momentum going.

'There was a series of meetings going on all over the place to do with gun and gang crime. We were finding that I might attend a meeting one day in Moss Side, and then the same meeting about the same issues was being held in Longsight the next day. The people running the meetings didn't know, so some of us started saying, "No, we need to coordinate all this." We decided to formulate a group and take all these questions to the police, to the Government and to the councillors. And we wanted the councillors to come to us and sit in on our meetings, not us going to their surgeries. Get the police to come to us and answer to us. These are our streets, our communities, our problems.'

CARISMA now works to take the voice of the grass roots to organisations and key stakeholders in the wider community, including Greater Manchester Police, Manchester City Council and the Home Office.

The issue of gangs and violent crime is one of the most serious challenges facing a number of our communities today. With traditional sources of authority under greater pressure than ever before, it has become increasingly important to find ways to support and strengthen parents, teachers and communities in their efforts to care for and develop young people, set clear boundaries and tackle antisocial behaviour. But as Erinma exemplifies, some of the communities most affected by such difficulties have also produced some of the most powerful voices for change, working to enable communities to support themselves.

Erinma's story is a key example, so relevant today, of how the greatest challenges we now face cannot be solved by government alone but only through a new partnership between government and the individuals and communities concerned. As her work shows, those nearest to the problems are so often closest to the solutions.

Erinma's husband, Raymond, is the co-founder of CARISMA, and together they have a busy life running their own childcare business. But a powerful connection and commitment to their community has led to them investing their time and considerable energies in tackling the issues that underlie local gun and gang crime. 'It's like a full-time job. It really is a lot of hard work. Me and my husband have cut our day job by two days a week so we can do our community work, which we're not getting paid for. But there is a passion to do this work, and someone's got to do it. Because I have the support of my community in what I do, that encourages me to continue.

'Together, me and my husband have eight children of our own, who are the same as those that are getting caught up out there on the streets. That really does spur me on. I honestly think that the parents of those children are no different from me, and I am no different from them. Any day my child could get caught up in something, but it's what I decide to do now and what I decide to instil in my child that will guide them in the opposite direction. It's the education I give my child that is important, not only the academic education they receive. For me, schooling is different from education. Education is what you get at home, it's what you get from the family, and it's about life issues. Schooling just gives you the technical bits to be able to get your GCSEs. You don't get a GCSE in street life. There's no such thing.'

The desire to prevent her children and others from making bad life choices has encouraged Erinma and the other members of the CARISMA team to search out practical ways to demonstrate that alternatives can be found for young people being drawn into street crime. 'We open different doors for them, let them see a different world. A lot of young people are brought up in inner-city and other urban environments. They don't get the opportunity to see outside that environment or to see what opportunities are available for them. They accept what they are given. If the perception is that they will not achieve, never be a lawyer or a doctor, but will end up getting involved in a gun gang, then it's that self-perpetuating thing: that's what they will do and that's what they will become. For these young people caught up in gun and gang crime, it's not what they want to do. They don't wake up in the morning and decide, "You know what, I'm going to get a gun today, and I'm going to go and shoot as many people as I can." There are different circumstances surrounding their lives that make them end up like that. We could actually do a lot of very good preventative work before they end up in the criminal justice system. By the time they are there, it is too late. We need to be doing things before they get involved, and there are things we can offer to young people. I let them know that, although I can't give them a job, I can put them in touch with someone else who might be able to offer them a job. And I tell them how they should present themselves when they go for an interview, offer to go with them: these are the kinds of things I can do.'

What particularly struck me about Erinma was the way she has channelled her anger and her concerns about the realities of life in her neighbourhood. Rather than giving in to fear, she works to ensure that the young people in her area are offered alternative visions of what their life could be like by, for example, visiting schools and leading assemblies. And rather than perpetuating a sense that her community was in crisis, she has worked to raise people's expectations of what their community could achieve and affirm the positive progress they can achieve together. 'If you want to see change,' she concludes, 'you must be part of the change.'

The most impressive example of this affirmation is Manchester Peace Week, now in its fifth year, and Erinma is rightly proud of its impact. CARISMA organises an annual week of events to express local people's desire for peace in Moss Side, Longsight and surrounding areas. The organisation stresses that peace is not just the absence of violence but also the building of secure communities where there is justice for all. Seeking to engage the whole community, the organisers emphasise that Peace Week is 'not about a few people doing everything; it is about everyone doing something'. Organisations, voluntary groups, businesses, faith groups and local people come together to celebrate what is good about their community.

'During the first Peace Week event, we invited parents, especially mothers, of young people that had been shot and killed, together with the families of those that had committed such crimes, in the hope that there could be a truce between the families. We decided if we could get all of them together and ask them to forgive each other – not to forget what's happened, because you can never forget, but to forgive – then that would be a way of moving forward and showing the other children in the families that they shouldn't carry this feud on any further. When we did the Peace Week march the following year, we approached the police and said we wanted to do a march – not a demonstration, a peaceful march – and we would like a police presence with us. Most importantly, we wanted the neighbourhoods that we were going to march through to see the police marching with us all for peace, as part of the community. That's how we built our good relationship with the police initially, and it continues. Now Peace Week is getting bigger and bigger every year: we go into schools and lead assemblies on peace; we run creative arts workshops, and the young children march with lanterns that they've made at school.'

Erinma is a powerful role model in her community, and, in many respects, the way she herself lives her life is as important in what she is trying to achieve as the many projects and campaigns she works on. 'If I can be a good simple role model, that's a good thing,' she says. 'I was born in Moss Side, just round the corner from where I live now. Went to the local primary school, the local secondary school and I do my local work in Moss Side. I feel that's a good role model, especially for the females out there. I can teach them a way to conduct themselves.'

Erinma, Raymond and the volunteers of CARISMA are striving to demonstrate that support and cooperation can replace fear and intimidation. They are evidence that those working for the good of their communities are the most powerful tool we have while striving to overcome the bad that can threaten our communities.

2

AVILA KILMURRAY

> There is knowledge, there is wisdom, in working-class
> communities, and it is a matter of tapping into those
> stories that very often aren't heard.

More than thirty years ago, at the height of the Troubles in Northern Ireland, Avila Kilmurray's flat was blown up. A student in Derry, she not only saw her flat destroyed but she also lost all her notes for the postgraduate thesis she was then trying to complete. 'As a twenty-two year old, I decided that I might as well see the Troubles out, thinking that would be about two years more, but I am still here!'

And so, in the mid-seventies, Avila's life took a new direction. A Catholic from Dublin, Avila got involved working with Loyalist communities in Derry. 'I felt that it was important to try to get into the thinking of those communities that you didn't know or easily understand. It's all too easy to just have your own values reinforced by working with communities that you do know and understand.'

Early on in her involvement, Avila realised something that has become a dominant feature of the work she now does. 'One of the things that came as a great shock to me was the amount of wisdom in local working-class communities. Not abstract academic knowledge but a much deeper sense of awareness of what the issues were, an awareness of what the problems were, and a fair idea of what to do about them, if they were given half a chance.'

This early insight – that local people are the experts in their own lives – is a recurring theme in Avila's work. 'In the particular situation of Northern Ireland in the 1970s, where, to an extent, normal society had broken down, it gave a space to liberate the capacity of local people to organise their own arrangements, their own alternative services, and an ability to articulate demands and negotiate with a whole range of different agencies in the Government and indeed with the paramilitaries. People were able to negotiate their own space for community action: that was a learning curve for me. There is knowledge, there is wisdom, in working-class communities, and it is a matter of tapping into those stories that very often aren't heard.'

Today, Avila Kilmurray is director of the Community Foundation for Northern Ireland, an independent grant-making organisation which aims to enable local activists working on both sides of the sectarian divide to drive social change and tackle social exclusion, poverty and social injustice. As well as its efforts in Northern Ireland, it also works to share its learning and support divided societies and societies emerging from conflict, from Africa to Asia to Latin America – right across the world.

I had the privilege three years ago of speaking at the twenty-fifth anniversary of the Community Foundation, formed in 1979. I was delighted to be able to announce that £6 million had been raised for its work and to be able to praise the unique achievements of Avila. A constant innovator and serial campaigner, Avila's extraordinary achievements at the foundation are just one strand of a remarkable career that has seen her make significant contributions to many developments which have changed the face of Northern Ireland over more than thirty years.

Sometimes it takes the people closest to the realities on the ground to see solutions where leaders and politicians often only see problems. In Northern Ireland, decades of conflict have at times left many struggling to find answers to seemingly intractable problems. But for Avila, a persistent belief in the ability of communities to solve their own problems has inspired a lifetime of quite remarkable service in pursuit of a better future for the communities of Northern Ireland.

While working in Derry during the 1970s, Avila also got involved in the emerging women's movement and was instrumental in setting up the first women's aid refuge there in 1977–8. 'We were told that domestic violence wasn't a problem. We actually squatted in a building to open a women's aid refuge. Peter Melchett, who was the Labour minister responsible for health and social services at the time, had to rescue us because we were denounced for being in breach of the emergency provisions legislation. He rang us and said, "I think you are in a bit of trouble; you had better come up and talk to us in Stormont." He gave us the building in the end. Sometimes you have to take action against what is the current common sense in order to move things forward. It's amazing what things are seen at any time as common sense, which in ten or twenty years people say, "Why was that believed?" We were denounced from the altar for breaking up marriages by opening up a women's aid refuge; that attitude has changed over the years.'

Avila told me about her work with the Northern Ireland Women's Coalition, which grew out of the community-based women's groups. 'Women were crucial, right through the Troubles, partially because they felt somewhat safer in terms of moving across the divides: they were slightly less likely to be shot. And partially because they always had that motivating factor of family: "What's going to happen to my children? I must do something to change the circumstances." The women's movement idea that the personal is political was common at the time.

'We basically tried to change the concept of politics. Rather than seeing politics or citizenship as a vote every four years,

29

instead of that it became, "How do we deconstruct politics so that it becomes more relevant?" We looked at who dictates what common sense is, what the norm is and what is off-the-wall. One of the things that we tried to do with the coalition was to come up with off-the-wall suggestions. For example, we came up with the idea of a nominated Civic Forum representing different sections of the community as the second chamber, rather than a senate or another House of Lords, and we got that into the Good Friday Agreement.'

Much of Avila's work has been to seek practical ways to link the separated communities of Northern Ireland. For example, the Community Foundation for Northern Ireland has attempted to find ways of bringing community representatives together to discuss issues of common concern. 'We used to talk about working within and between communities. We would use the "commonality of issues" approach to bring people together in a non-threatening situation. That means, if we were funding twenty groups all working around women's issues, they would come together at a women's conference. Or if a number of groups were employing a worker for the first time, you bring them together to talk about employment duties and responsibilities. In doing that, we were also creating a situation where these people could come together. People were divided by physical peace lines, so we were always looking for the niches where you could bring people together.'

The challenges that Avila has encountered for so many years may to many have seemed insurmountable. But as Avila passionately explains, it is her belief in the potential and the ability of people to solve problems for themselves that has motivated and inspired her. 'If this is about inclusive society, then it's important to give the voice and the power of definition to the people that are excluded, and not to the people who are dictating to them why they are excluded. I hate people talking about "capacity building" and all the rest. I was listening recently to Professor Muhammad Yunus, founder of the Grameen Bank, and he talked about "liberating potential", saying that human beings are programmed with potential and it's a matter of liberating it, not someone else doling out "capacity building" to people like a dose of medicine.'

Despite her extraordinary achievements, Avila rejected the idea that her serial activism might be identified as an inspiration to others. 'I wouldn't see myself as inspirational, because you always do things in small groups or in talking to one or two people. It's unusual for one person to have an idea and go ahead with it. Actually, in general, we would tend to be a bit suspect if that was the case; many people work very well in small groups, not as individual leaders. Success happens when you have the ability to throw an idea around.'

She did, however, readily identify others who have influenced her. 'There are so many people I have found inspirational in so many ways. I met the late Cathy Harkin when I first went to Derry. She had done really well at school but had had to leave at fifteen due to poverty and go to work at the Shorts factory. She had been involved in the civil-rights movement and Derry Labour Party. She was completely inspirational to me. She was so human; she would talk to people and immediately know what the issues were. It was the pair of us that were involved in setting up the Derry women's aid refuge. With Cathy, there were no mental boundaries: one minute she would be negotiating about the women's aid refuge, the next minute she would be talking about the history of women in Derry, the suffragettes, and linking politics, economics and changes in society. Too often we can get ourselves into silos about economics or politics or whatever; she taught me that it is all tied up together and it is mad to separate it.'

Looking back, Avila says there has been in Northern Ireland 'a breaking of the silence. Twenty-five years ago, when we started, we had to work amidst violence and try to normalise things. It's remarkable that from what were twenty-five years ago the ten most deprived areas with paramilitary gatekeepers, local women have gone to South Africa, met people there and returned to raise money from this relatively poor community for a South African Aids orphanage. Now from Northern Ireland we can look outwards and help others.'

Today, Avila is still thinking of new ways of improving local communities – conflict-resolution work, tackling immigration issues, building greater women's involvement – and still providing the mechanisms for local communities to bring their wisdom to bear on the issues they experience. 'One of the things that I'm looking at at the moment is how you can actually look forward and see issues happening – like migration, that could well lead to racism – so you can take preventative action, learning from other societies, rather than waiting till it's a crisis and it's turning into riots and then take remedial action, which is never as effective. I'm also looking at how you can work – even in the midst of conflict – to try and maintain links and see where there are pulse points for change, and to give a voice to people so that they then can be part of the solution.'

3

ANNE GLOVER

*What the statistics and all the findings and all the
outputs and outcomes don't say is just how much
you can actually change somebody's life.*

I've been to Leicester several times in recent months, and
after travelling to Braunstone, a community in the city, I
visited the home of Anne Glover, a leading local activist,
local councillor and vice-chair of the Braunstone Community
Association (BCA), a resident-led neighbourhood renewal
company. As I had coffee with her and her friends, I heard
the remarkable story of her devotion to her local community
and how, as a result of her efforts to chase out drugs and
drug dealers and to stop antisocial behaviour, she has had to
withstand personal threat, harassment and intimidation.

Anne's family have lived in Braunstone for five generations –
all raised, schooled, living and working there. 'My grandparents
moved onto the estate in 1933. We're now on our fifth
generation, and we're all still here: my whole family live within
a mile of my house. It's one of the reasons I got involved in my
community.' This long-standing history connects her strongly
to her local area, and she knows that her family's prospects are
bound up with those of her neighbours and her community.
Her commitment to her community is a natural extension of
her desire to build a better future for her grandchildren.

As Anne told me her story, I was struck by how a person
who is now such a key figure within her community had never

seen herself as a leader and might never have chosen to get involved had someone not invited her to take the first step.

Anne left school with no qualifications and worked in shops and factories until, about ten years ago, she had quite a serious accident that left her disabled. One day, whilst she was at home unable to work due to her accident, Anne noticed a gathering at her local community centre. 'I lived over the road from one of our community buildings. I saw all these cars parked outside, so I hurried down to the centre. I was about to go in when I saw people's names being ticked off a list, and I thought it must be invitees only. I turned to leave when somebody stopped me. She said, "Are you a resident? Come in, come in, we'd love you to be here."'

The meeting concerned the development of the New Deal for Communities (NDC) pathfinder scheme. The local area had been awarded significant funds for regeneration. 'The neighbourhood that I live in, Braunstone, was identified as being in the top 10 per cent for severe deprivation. I went in to the meeting, and they were talking about how we were going to spend the money – on community projects and so on. It was announced that nothing would be spent without the residents' say-so. Well, at the time, there were only half a dozen residents in this crowded room. You could tell because we were the most scruffily dressed – we stuck out like sore thumbs! But we became the most popular people in that room – they were all queuing up to tell us about their ideas on how they wanted to spend our money.'

Seeing how central residents themselves were to be to the new scheme, this first meeting sparked Anne's enthusiasm. She became involved at this early stage of what was to become Braunstone Community Association, a resident-led neighbourhood renewal company established to manage the £49.5 million the area had been allocated under the New Deal for Communities programme. Anne's first role in the BCA was as a project appraiser. 'I'll never forget the first project that I ever appraised. It was a proposal to have extra police in the area, because our crime rate was through the ceiling. They said they were going to send the inspector. I looked out the window and said, "Oh no, they've sent some young bobby", but he *was* the inspector! I've always been told you're old when the police start looking young. He was a really nice man and we approved this project.'

Following her introduction to local crime-prevention issues, Anne's involvement in this and other areas soon became much more hands-on. Anne told me about how, realising the damage being caused by a prolific drug dealer operating in her own street, she made up her mind she would tackle the problem. 'We set about getting this person removed. The biggest problem was getting witnesses to come forward to say this person was dealing drugs. I was prepared to come forward as a witness, and originally there were twenty-five of us who were going to go forward. We even organised a meeting away from the estate so that people didn't know it was going on, but on the night, I was the only one who turned up. All the rest had been intimidated and didn't go. When it went to court, I was still the only one that turned up.

'I started to have a lot of harassment at that time. I had my car fire-bombed, I had my windows in my house put through, and I had paint chucked all over the house. When I got my new car, they screwdrivered it all down one side, and this was all because I was a witness against this drug dealer.'

In the face of such intimidation, Anne continued to stand up against the threats, and finally she saw the improvements she'd been fighting for. 'Eventually, the drug dealer was evicted and straightaway the area changed. We used to have burnt-out cars every night, kids used to be on the street, because the drug dealer attracted all sorts of people. But the worst of it was that drugs were sold to such young people, and their only means of getting income was to turn to crime. I was burgled six times myself and so were my neighbours. In fact, in a row of eight houses, I was the only one still there: everyone else had gone. I stood firm. I flatly refused to move. I said, "No, I'm not letting them drive me out of my house." They've won if you do that.'

Anne was determined to tackle the things that were bringing her neighbourhood down. But creating a lasting improvement in the area meant not just addressing those issues that were driving people out but also focusing on what would bring people into the area and give it a new lease of life. Now vice-chair of the BCA, Anne's work has grown in scale and aspiration. 'We took over 250 houses that the local authority was going to pull down because nobody would live in them, practically every one empty and boarded up. There was a waiting list to move out of Braunstone. The Braunstone Community Association took them off the council at a pound each and, working with a housing association, spent £10 million doing them up. I even put my own name down for one of the disabled bungalows. Now there is a waiting list of two years to move into Braunstone because we've transformed the area so much.'

Today in Braunstone, housing, health, public safety and employment prospects are all being improved as a result of the resident-led regeneration. The work has had its fair share of difficulties, and Anne was very honest about the good times and the bad but always resolute in her focus. 'I think the main reason we succeeded is because, even though we've hit our bumpy roads and we've had fallouts, we never lost sight of what it was we were trying to do, and we stood firm. We've done projects to get people back into work. We've got our own job centre on the estate. We've done a teenage-pregnancy project. We've done a fitness and healthy-eating project. We've built a health centre and a youth house.'

But among all these notable successes, Anne is particularly inspired by the BCA's efforts to raise the bar for what young people in the area might expect from their future. 'We started a project called "University of the First Age", because nobody ever talked to our kids about their aspirations. Nobody ever asked, "Would you like to go to university after school?" Now we give a £2,000 bursary to each student that goes to university, for them to buy books, IT equipment or even just to pay for their living expenses. We've got a young woman at Cambridge University that we sponsor.'

Anne didn't set out to turn her neighbourhood around, but she saw an opportunity to get involved, and she put herself forward. Over the years, her involvement has grown and with it her confidence about just how much can be achieved by local residents determined to create the kind of neighbourhood they want for their families. Anne has given so much of herself, and, in doing so, she has gained so much, too.

'I won't deny that it's not been easy; I'm still learning. People say to me, "Why do you do it?" and I think for me the biggest reason is that when I was first disabled, I thought, "What do I do now?" Life does sort of take a downward spiral, but this work has given me a new direction. I feel it is a reason for me to get out of bed in the mornings. What am I most proud of? I think the work I've done with the BCA. What the statistics and all the findings and all the outputs and outcomes don't say is just how much you can actually change somebody's life. There's my own, I know that for a kick-off, but the lives of other people in the community have also been completely transformed, and it's all because somebody understood the problems and was able to help them onto the first step on the ladder, because we took away all the barriers. It's been achieved by a lot of people doing a lot of hard work: local people doing it voluntarily.'

It might seem like a natural place to begin, but often working to improve your own community, or trying to tackle those problems closest to home, can require real courage. When the problems you want to address are affecting your own streets and neighbours, you can't get involved by halves or care from a distance. As I have seen with many neighbourhood activists, those who try and make changes from within often risk the most. But in having the courage to take these risks and to stand up in defence of a better future, local activists across the country are sowing the seeds of change.

Even when the odds were against her, Anne always had faith in her local community, and they recently expressed their faith in her by electing her as a local councillor. Anne's long history in this neighbourhood means she more than anyone knows the consequences of community deprivation and decline. And, more importantly, she more than anyone has a stake in the benefits of community renewal and transformation. In Anne's words, it's simple: 'My motivation is that I'm the third generation of my five generations, I've got four and five that come after me, and I want to make sure for them and other people's families that the area continues to prosper.'

4

PETER MORSON

*I've had my say, and now we want the young ones
to come and say what they want to do . . . because
after all it's their world, it's going to be their village.*

I met Peter Morson when I visited the small ex-mining village
of Dordon in Warwickshire. For years, Peter worked down
the mines. Today, he chairs the parish council and is a borough
councillor.

As I have travelled the country, I have met many men and
women who have devoted their lives to their local community
and made a huge difference. Peter's story is one of the most
powerful illustrations of just how much can be achieved by
local heroes devoted to improving their communities.

When I visited Dordon, Peter, who has already helped
to transform employment opportunities in the area, was
embarking on yet another new project: bringing the whole
community together to tackle antisocial behaviour. His latest
innovative efforts include a plan to provide young people with
improved youth facilities while at the same time clamping
down heavily on antisocial behaviour with new policing
measures.

As a young man, Peter began work with the main local
employer, Birch Coppice Quarry, which at its peak employed
about 1,800 people. The majority of local people worked at
the colliery, and the pit closures of the 1980s left a big void
in Dordon. Most of the miners lost their jobs and the area

39

suffered from unemployment and neglect. Peter recalled, 'We had an estate here which was built by the Coal Board for the miners. People that were living there, I think they felt a bit dejected. The kids would move outside North Warwickshire to all the conurbations around us. We're a mass exporter of workers: those that can, go elsewhere. The ones that were left felt a bit downgraded.'

During these years, Dordon not only suffered a decline in opportunities for work but also felt the impact of rising aspirations amongst local young people for a better standard of life. 'Most of the kids now are getting better educated: they're beginning to understand the extra choices that people want. When I left school, I had two choices in life: I could either go on to university, if my dad paid for it, or I went to the pit. Now young people want something out of life, opportunities need to be there. If they're not, young people move, and that's what's happened: many have gone, they've moved out.'

Witnessing the changing circumstances of his village and inspired by a strong sense of duty, Peter wanted to get something done. 'I was brought up to care for people and to look after those that can't look after themselves. I can't do everything for everybody, but I do my best to see what I can do for them. I'm well known in the village, I've lived here all my life. I used to know the parents, I know the mothers, I know the grannies, but I passionately care about people. I think there's good in everybody, and I do the best I can for them.

'I was mayor in 1993–4. One of my pet projects was to regenerate the colliery site to create some jobs there. Run-down areas get blighted with antisocial behaviour: people don't care and everything starts to go to rack and ruin. I went on the radio and said we wanted some decent-quality jobs.' Thanks in part to Peter's campaigning, a major regeneration scheme has developed new industrial and retail units on the former colliery sites and created more than 1,000 jobs for local people, with the potential of further growth. 'What that's done to the village, it's given it a boost. It lifts everybody up to know that at least they can work. There's nothing worse than to think you've been chucked out, because many of us were unskilled and didn't know what else we could do. But people have found skills that they didn't realise they had. So the village has actually reinvented itself since then.'

As well as working to ensure local employment opportunities, Peter has used his position on the local parish council and borough council to develop several local initiatives aimed at regenerating community facilities. 'The play park was under water most of the time, so we had a new one built and a kickabout park. We regenerated the village hall, because we realised that people need a focal point. It's very well used by all groups at the moment. We find it difficult to fit our parish council meetings in sometimes because it's booked up. And we've created a country park at the bottom of Birch Coppice and stocked the fishing pools up as another leisure facility. Eventually the big pit mound will be planted and become a woodland walk.'

Peter's commitment to his village has been a major part of his life for many years. As life has brought its celebrations and its challenges, its joys and its difficulties, he has continued in his work, finding strength amidst his community, which has seen him through tough times. Peter's youngest son, Danny, was born with some complications: 'He had the cord round his neck. When he was eighteen months, he was diagnosed with a hole in the heart. Between two years old and twelve, over ten years, he had seven heart operations to put him right. He went through agony. Anyway, they finally got him right. He was pretty weedy, then all of a sudden he shot up, he grew to 6 ft 3 in. Unfortunately, Danny was killed a few years ago in a car crash when he was twenty-one, in 1998. Everybody liked him in the village. I've never known him miserable; he was always happy. I must admit I do miss him. He'd do anything for anybody. I think he'd have been a politician and all if he was still alive.'

Peter's work with the young people of Dordon has been inspired by Danny's memory. 'When we were picking our play equipment for the new park, Danny said to me, "Dad, are you sure that the kids want that?" I said, "What do you mean, son?" He said, "I'll tell you summat, they probably won't." So we had a proper election round at the primary school for all the kids to pick what they wanted. And it's been the least vandalised equipment throughout the borough, because there's ownership of it. The kids say, "I got that."'

Danny's awareness of the importance of getting young people involved in developing youth provision and facilities has inspired Peter and the council to embark on some innovative solutions for local youth needs, with the young people themselves at the centre. 'We happened to be having one of our council surgeries at our village hall, and some of the young people were there. They came in and asked us if we could do something for them, which I thought was excellent. We said, "What do you want?" and went through it. We arranged a meeting with Mike O'Brien, the MP, myself, county councillors and youth workers, and discussed what we were going to do. We came up with a six-point plan.'

The agreed plan is an interesting model, involving the county youth services, the police and the parish council in joint efforts to tackle antisocial behaviour and improve opportunities for young people. It includes expectations of behaviour change, an increase in police surveillance and enforcement, and the establishment of a new facility for local young people. 'They wanted somewhere that they could call their own, and I totally agree with them. I said, "What would you like?" and then we came up with the POD, as it's called: the Positive Operational Drop-In. I don't know who invented that one! It's a mobile building that comes ready equipped with everything: tables, chairs, and it's got its own generator. We spoke to the kids and asked them where they wanted the POD. They gave us three suggestions, and we've picked one of them: that's part of their ownership of it.'

The plan is already yielding results: youth workers are staffing the POD and engaging young people, asking them what they want provided; there are fewer young people hanging around with nothing to do; and CCTV is improving community safety. But for Peter, the youth plan was not an end in itself but just the beginning of new efforts to increase the engagement of young people in local democracy. 'We've got to talk to the people. We've got to engage them, got to give them some responsibility. We've realised that young people need a voice, so we set up our parish youth council. They've had voting down at the high school, and they've elected eight members and appointed a chair. She's sixteen years old and she wants something done! I'm just sorting out the constitution with them, and once that's done they will formulate what they want to do for the young people of Dordon. They're learning about the council, they're learning about citizenship. In the future, they'll be parish councillors, county councillors, MPs even.'

Today, many are concerned about perceived political apathy and falling electoral turnout, and they are right to be, for an active democracy relevant to every citizen is a fundamental prerequisite for any efforts to build a better society. As many stories in this book illustrate, these very real concerns are being tackled by the innovative efforts of those seeking to encourage new expressions of citizen engagement and new mechanisms for democratic participation. But I also wanted to celebrate here the willing commitment of thousands of elected representatives in our borough councils and town councils and parish councils, who give of their time freely to serve our communities. Once the party rosettes have been packed away and the electioneering is over, men and women from all political convictions set to work to serve their communities and argue the case for what they believe to be right for their constituents. While the media spotlight may focus on Westminster, we must never forget that the very heart of British democracy is being supported and renewed every day by people working in town halls, civic centres and village halls, administering and improving their communities.

Peter is continually looking for new ways to help, new ways to make life a little bit better for those in his village. And while the impact of all his efforts is clear to see, for Peter, working to improve life in his community is not heroic, it's just the natural thing to do. Peter's time on the parish and county councils hasn't always been easy, but his sense of responsibility is inspiring. He wanted a better future for his village, for his neighbours, and he put himself forward to be a part of the change he wanted to see. And now, he wants others to take up the challenge. 'For twenty years, I've been a politician here. At my age I've had my say, and now we want the young ones to come and say what they want to do, how they want to change it, because after all it's their world, it's going to be their village, they've got to deal with it.'

5

SUSAN LANGFORD

Both young and older people are generally underestimated by society . . . not listened to or noticed enough. I think the strength of intergenerational work is that it looks at what people can do rather than what they can't do.

All round the country I hear the same concern: worries from older people that young people never talk to them and questions from young people about why older people don't understand them.

Susan Langford has an explanation – and a solution. 'The reason is that all those informal places where young and old used to meet and interact no longer exist. You're unlikely to see old people with young people, and yet put them in a room together and they realise they're fundamentally the same and they understand what they have in common.'

So, to bridge the generation gap, Susan Langford founded Magic Me, an organisation based in London's East End that has the aim of bringing young and older people together in joint arts projects. And such has been her success that she has even seen pensioners and young students studying and then passing citizenship GCSEs together, including two pensioners who had never sat an exam in their lives.

It was after her training and early work in graphic design that Susan became interested in community arts: a broad term that means finding ways to use the visual arts to bring people together in the community – to build relationships at the same time as creating artwork. 'I met a women called Kathy Levin, who was in England talking about her work in America, which she called "intergenerational". She had set up Magic Me in Baltimore. It just sounded intriguing – it was taking young people, children at risk, into nursing homes with the aim of setting up a structure where the two groups could work together to create something. I was very intrigued and tried running some pilot projects in London.'

These attempts to bring young and older people together for shared learning and creativity encouraged Susan to set up Magic Me in London in 1989. And while Levin's model inspired her, she was particularly driven by what she had seen in her work in care homes for older people. 'I was shocked by the grimness of these places and the sense of isolation, despair and sadness experienced by the residents. A sense of injustice drove my desire to change that environment. I wanted to bring the real world into those spaces and to help the people there to continue their life experiences. It felt like people went into care and then really quickly went downhill; they just didn't have anything going on in their life.'

Susan remembers one individual in particular who confirmed her belief in the importance of this work and whose memory continues to inspire her. 'Very early on, through a project with a local junior school, I met a woman called Rose who has always been an inspiration for me. She was Jewish; she grew up in Whitechapel, in the East End of London. She told me about her life as a child, roaming around and being a trouble to the people who ran the market stalls. She wanted to talk about her Jewish background: recognising she was at the end of her life, it was important for her to know who she was. I only knew her for about three months before she died. I found out when her funeral was and decided to go along. I was the only person who was there. She'd lived for eighty-seven years, and I'd only known her for three months. I thought there was something completely wrong there. When I arrived, the care home had messed up and booked a Christian burial for Rose. I witnessed what I thought was total hypocrisy and just said goodbye to Rose in my own way. The sense of how wrong that was stayed with me. Somebody's whole identity was negated. It seemed like she'd been eradicated, that people had forgotten who she'd been for all those years. They'd lost sight of how a community is woven together, and if we lose sight of how a community works – and the place of both young and old people within it – then we all lose out, really.'

Susan has spent twenty years working to bring young and older people together, finding ways for each to share, learn from and build upon each other's experiences, beliefs and identities. In a multicultural society, and a society of rapid social change, the forces that divide young and old, that divide those of different cultures and religions, must be overcome by those working to build bridges and bring people together. Susan's work is so profound because it is driven not by a fear of division or polarisation but by a wonder and curiosity about people, a desire to celebrate the uniqueness of individual experience, and a belief in the huge amount every individual has to give and to gain from sharing their uniqueness with those who are different from them.

She explains the Magic Me model: 'Magic Me is an arts organisation, it's also a community development organisation and a charity. We run arts projects that get young people and older people working together. It might be learning photography and putting on an exhibition; it might be writing poetry together and publishing a small book; it might be drama, music . . . anything. A mixed group of young and older people come together with a shared purpose and in the process find out something about one another. I think the gap between young and older people is bigger now because the informal times and places that people used to meet, bump into each other and get to know each other have gone because people move around so much now, communities are so mobile. So what we are trying to do is create those spaces ourselves.

'Every project we do has three aims. One is creative: "Let's make a book, or let's learn artistic skills by working with professional artists." The second is about personal development, which is where the title "Magic Me" comes in. This is about giving people confidence to go into a difficult situation and learn things about themselves. And then the third is about community development: "How can I feel more comfortable about people who are different from me in my community? How can I engage with the other generations so that I don't stand at the bus stop being afraid of young people or cursing them?"'

While Magic Me now works across London, the particular nature of the East End, its home and focus, is key to understanding what Susan is setting out to achieve. 'The particular thing that's going on in the whole of London, but very markedly in this borough, is that the generations are very different culturally and ethnically. The school population is about 70 per cent Bangladeshi Muslim young people, whereas the seventy-plus generation is about 70 per cent white indigenous older people. People have lots of questions: "How do I connect with my neighbours? Are they going to speak my language? Why do they wear those clothes?" These are the kinds of questions that people have, but there is nowhere to meet where they can ask the questions and start the conversations. We offer a safe place, and we invite people *because* they're different. It makes it easier to start a conversation: "Oh, you're different to me. Let's talk about it." You find the similarities as well. "We live down the same road" or "We both support Arsenal", or whatever the shared concern is. It might be they're both worried that there's drug dealing on our estate, and that's no different if you're a Bangladeshi seventeen year old or if you're an eighty year old. We are creating a place and structures for people to find what their commonalities are and take pride in their differences.'

The stories of Magic Me's diverse and fascinating projects speak for themselves and are the best way to understand what their unique approach is achieving. 'We did a project with Mulberry School for Girls, which has about 98 per cent Bangladeshi Muslim students although it's a state school, and local older women, none of whom were Bangladeshi or Muslim but were African, white, Jewish and Christian. Together, they looked at the story of the suffragettes and what women were prepared to die for, or to be starved for, or locked up for, and how they campaigned. Together, they thought about what issues they would go and campaign for or campaign against. By talking about those issues, they were able to explore attitudes like, "I'll stick my neck out and wear a headscarf in public even if people shout at me sometimes." One of the turning points for the young women was when they realised the older women had the same feelings as them about the Iraq War. They expected that all older white people would be in favour of the war, but they discovered that most of the older women were completely against it – and against any war, because they've lived through wars and the Jewish women had experienced prejudice. They had experienced the same feelings as the young Muslim women and found a lot of common ground.'

What Susan's stories demonstrate is the absolute power of personal experiences and encounters as an educational tool and as an unsurpassed way to make people confront their assumptions and prejudices and open their minds to new possibilities. 'We meet people and whether they're seventeen or they're seventy-three they've had a long time getting to where they are and a lot of influences on them. But it can be remarkable how the experience of working closely with another person can make someone change their mind or just open up: "I have very strong beliefs but so does the lady in front of me. And actually what we have in common is that we have very strong beliefs." So I think it's about gaining a new perspective: "Sometimes other people have a point of view that doesn't eradicate mine." And I suppose people take that with them after the project has finished.'

One story in particular sums up so much of what Susan's innovative approach has been able to achieve, the way it has touched lives, and the diverse – and sometimes unexpected – range of outcomes that are evidence of its success. 'We worked with Oaklands Secondary School and Sundial Older People's Centre. The school had a group of students studying for a GCSE in citizenship. Part of the course was doing something in the community, and they asked Magic Me to get involved. I talked to the older people about it and asked if they would get involved in a project about what it means to be a good citizen in Bethnal Green. They bought the idea, but they said, "The young people are going to take a GCSE, so what are we going to get out of this?" I said, "You can do the GCSE as well, if you like!"

'Four of the older people sat their GCSEs. They had to go in the school hall and sit in the rows behind 120 fifteen year olds. I think I was the most nervous parent on exam-result day. I was down at the school with them, and they all passed, and all the young people passed: it was absolutely wonderful. Two of the men had never taken an exam before. One had left school at twelve. He'd been a refugee from France at the beginning of the Second World War. He never got on at school. His school got bombed one night, and the children were told to go to another school, but he never went and nobody ever asked after him. So, aged seventy-seven, he finally got a certificate. That was really fantastic. It made a real impact on the young people, too: seeing people who didn't have to learn but wanted to. Within the school, I think it really changed some of the teachers' minds about what working with older people is about: they suddenly realised there was more to this. So they've done other projects. They are reviewing their timetable, and they want to build Magic Me into that so every year there's a project that's part of a life-skills course. It feels like it's really got through that tangible educational gains can be made from working with older people.'

With gentleness and determination in equal measure, Susan has built a powerful model that is breaking down prejudice, building connections and touching lives. Susan reflected on what has made Magic Me so successful and why it has meant so much to the individuals and organisations it has worked with. 'The people we work with feel that both young and older people are generally underestimated by society, that they are not listened to or noticed enough. I think the strength of intergenerational work is that it looks at what people can do rather than what they can't do. So often, provision, particularly for older people, is about what they need and what they lack, whereas actually what they've got is an incredible amount of talent and skill and energy and time. And the same goes for young people. It's not just about providing youth services where they can come and do stuff but about harnessing their energies. How do we look at people in terms of what they bring rather than what they need?'

The wider lessons are clear: 'Government and local government and commerce divide people up into age groups. They provide services like that. Consumerism is all age related, so twenty-one year olds to twenty-four year olds buy this phone, and then the next group want something else. We need to think more coherently about how those things add up together. How do we provide for people in ways that bring people together rather than dividing them up?'

6

PAUL BAIN

You don't end up with a drug problem or a drink problem and on the streets over two or three months. It can take ten or twelve years to reach that position, and it will take you that long to get back.

W hat inspires a couple who are successful public servants to give up their careers and home and spend their whole lives living with and supporting homeless people? That's what Paul, a policeman, and his wife Jane, a nurse, did fifteen years ago, and they have been running a community for homeless men and women ever since.

As Paul explained to me, they were inspired by the idea of community and by how innovations in collective living could help house and befriend the homeless, and as a result they founded a new and unique community in Cambridge. Choosing to change their lives for an experiment they believed in, they didn't just give of their time or money, they didn't just choose to volunteer or even to take on a new job. Paul and Jane chose to give everything: living, working, eating with and being fully part of the community they were trying to build for others.

'We were both working within the public sector,' Paul told me. 'I was a policeman in Cambridge, and my wife Jane was a nurse. Both of us were brought up in the late fifties and early sixties, when ideas of living life differently were being espoused. We were attracted by the idea of living within a commune or a kibbutz, where, rather than generating your own wealth, you actually generate wealth for a body and all of you share in it. That was a style of living that Jane and I have always looked to as well worth a try.

'We saw an advert in a local paper saying: "If you're concerned about homelessness and unemployment, come along to this open meeting and discuss a new way to deal with both of them."' The meeting was held by Emmaus, an international charity formed more than fifty years ago in France that works predominantly with people who are homeless. The Emmaus approach is to bring people together to live within a community, living together and supporting each other, sharing meals and household jobs, and working in the community business. As Paul explained, they were captivated. 'We'd both been involved with other organisations that were dealing with people who were marginalised. This was like a breath of fresh air. It was an organisation that was set up to do something rather than just talking about things. An organisation that was all about rolling up your sleeves, getting your hands dirty and doing something that was going to alleviate people's problems there and then. People are brought back into a community of their own rather than existing on the outside.'

Many of the stories in this book highlight the power of community as a force for changing lives. Our community is the space where we join together with others, bound by shared interests or simply our shared humanity: the space where we become more than a collection of individuals and where we can achieve more together than we could alone. And for those of us lucky enough to be a part of a strong and caring community, it is where we go to share our joys and to seek help during times of need. Paul and Jane's story in particular spoke to me of the power of a community to enable people to imagine new realities and to become better versions of themselves.

Whilst still working full time, Paul and Jane, along with others, volunteered their time to establish the first Emmaus community in the UK. 'A site was bought. It was an old county council farm with nothing on it at all apart from a couple of wrecked cowsheds. Ourselves and a group of volunteers set to clearing the site and getting things going.'

As the project developed over the next year, discussions began over who was going to lead the new community. For Paul and Jane, the invitation came as quite a surprise. 'Out of the blue, myself and my wife were offered the opportunity to go over to France to visit three or four communities over a weekend. When we came back, we were asked if we wanted the job. We said yes – and then thought about it!'

Part of the ethos of Emmaus is that people who oversee communities live in the community on a full-time basis. So, Paul and Jane sold their house, moved into the Emmaus premises and took on the role of leading the emerging community and working with companions: the term used for the homeless individuals who come to live within the community. The community supports itself by collecting, refurbishing and selling furniture and other household goods no longer needed by their owners.

Becoming part of Emmaus Cambridge is not an easy option for companions. When they join, they agree to sign off state benefits and work for forty hours a week in the community. Emmaus supports them as they address the many complex needs they come with – with drug abuse having now overtaken alcohol abuse as the biggest problem for those joining the community. They also make a commitment to the shared ethos of 'helping others to live, grow and find dignity through sharing, work and self-respect'. These conditions of joining are the way in which the community expresses its belief in individuals' capacity to make changes in their lives. Paul is insistent that it is only by really believing that anyone can change that you give them the opportunity to change, and that if you have high expectations, you encourage people to rise to meet your expectations. 'You get people that come to the community who other organisations won't touch with a bargepole because they're violent, they have drink problems, drug problems, and they've been through the mill, time after time after time. The door is shut firmly against them. We don't believe that they can't be helped. We believe that, given the right set of circumstances, people can change. That has been proved time and time again with us. Myself and Jane are still in overall charge of what happens here, but the day-to-day running and 95 per cent of what happens now is dealt with by a leadership team predominantly made up of people who came here with drink and drug problems.'

Founding the first Emmaus community was an experiment, and like all experiments it has brought unexpected successes and unexpected challenges. But Paul speaks with real satisfaction when he describes the journey the community has gone on. 'We now have a very successful community. Over fifteen years, we have been able to help over 500 people. We were the first one in the UK; there are now thirteen communities. We had a definite idea of what we believed an Emmaus community should be, and we were allowed to do it. We had a trustee group who were very involved. Emmaus was such a revolutionary idea, such an unusual idea, that it caught many people's imaginations in those early years.'

The setbacks, however severe, have in their own way proved to be vital building blocks in the community's development. 'There are things that haven't worked, and I think it's important that the impression isn't given that everything has been a huge success. One of the ideas is that you bring companions on so that they eventually run the community. We knew that was going to be difficult, but we didn't realise it was going to be as difficult as it turned out to be. This is very much a 24/7 job, and in the first couple of years we really didn't get any time off. We eventually took a week's holiday, leaving somebody in charge who we felt was capable of standing in for us when we went away. Unfortunately, he, in conjunction with two other companions, took the safe, nicked the car and caused all sorts of problems. We involved the police, and the community was very, very unsettled. From being a community of a dozen we went down to a community of probably four, because obviously some people went when the crime was committed.

'The important thing was that we were then able to explain to the trustees the idea that Emmaus is an ongoing process. It isn't something where someone comes, they mess up once, and the door is shut and they're never allowed back. Once the case had been to court, we said, "Look, we're not here for retribution, we are here because this money was taken. It doesn't belong to us; it's the property of the charity and that needs to be repaid. As soon as these people finish the court case, they will be welcome to come back into the community again." And in welcoming them back, the keys of the safe were slapped back in their hands again, and we said, "Look, if you want to do this again then you go ahead and do it, but you've got to understand that this isn't some soulless body that you're taking the money from. It's the people you live, eat, sleep and work with. Those that you work with day by day are going to suffer, nobody else." It was very difficult persuading the trustees that that was what should happen. But it did happen.'

Learning from the good times and the bad has allowed Paul to approach his work with both hope and realism, both an unshakeable belief in people's capacity for change and the patience and persistence that comes from knowing it's never going to be easy. 'It's what Emmaus is about. It's about saying, "You guys that come to us may have ended up on the street, but you have a past somewhere that didn't involve that." You don't end up with a drug problem or a drink problem and on the streets over two or three months. It can take ten or twelve years to reach that position, and it will take you that long to get back. The idea that you'll get taken from the streets into a night shelter, into a hostel, into a flat within a period of six months and everything will be hunky-dory: well, it just doesn't happen.'

The founder of Emmaus, Abbé Pierre, has been a key inspiration to Paul and Jane in their ambitious experiment. 'He was a French priest who had a fairly privileged background, a member of the French Resistance and an excellent forger, providing papers to escape the Nazis. His name was Henri Grouès, but Abbé Pierre was the name that he was known by in the Resistance, and he kept that when he found fame after the war and became a member of the French parliament. He had a house that came with the job of being a priest, which was falling down around his ears. Someone turned up on his doorstep one day, and he let them in on the condition that they did the house up. Word got round and more people turned up at his door, so he tore down the huts that had been used to house prisoners of war and put them in his back garden, and gradually built up these communities around Paris.

'In the severe winter of 1954, people were freezing to death all over France. He was informed of a case of a woman who had been evicted by a landlord and was found frozen to death the following morning on the doorstep, clutching the eviction notice. He forced his way into what was then the Radio Luxembourg studio, grabbed the microphone and shamed the people of France into what's known as a "revolution of goodness". He let them know what was going on and received millions of francs to carry on his work.

'It was a real privilege to have met him four or five times. While there were difficulties communicating because his English wasn't very good and my French is non-existent, language isn't always essential in a meeting of minds, I think.'

Paul and Jane have dedicated their lives to turning this man's vision into a model of community. Motivated by their achievements, others have spread the Emmaus model across the country. What makes this model so powerful is that, while many services for the homeless and unemployed focus on their needs, their problems, or what they lack, Emmaus focuses on what they have to give, as responsible members of a community, supporting each other.

In Paul's words, Abbé Pierre was 'a man who was known for his piety, but he wouldn't see it that way. He would just see the fact that he was an ordinary human being, just doing his job in supporting other human beings to get through hard times.' A very fitting tribute to Paul and Jane themselves.

7

BRUCE CROWTHER

Nothing I'm doing is any better than what others are doing, but it's an example. This is what's being replicated all over the country.

Think of a town where just about every trader supports Fairtrade and where just about every citizen plays their part. And think of the town that invented the idea of Fairtrade Towns, the first in the world.

Garstang is an ordinary small market town in Lancashire. Its population is little more than 5,000. But in recent years, Garstang has become a symbol for what can be achieved by those fighting for a more just world. Because in 2000, and thanks to the work of a group of local campaigners led by local vet Bruce Crowther, Garstang became the world's first Fairtrade Town.

Ninety of the town's one hundred traders sell or use Fairtrade products, three of the town's five cafés are now Fairtrade cafés, and the town has twinned with the cocoa-farming community of New Koforidua in Ghana and is planning to develop a direct trading link between the two towns.

Like many campaigners, Bruce's involvement in the trade-justice agenda dates back to his time as a student – and to one seminal event: the Band Aid record which led to the Live Aid concert. 'What Bob Geldof did was absolutely fantastic. He was outraged by what he saw, and he did what he could to stop it. The point is that many people do that sort of thing, but

he could pick up a phone and get Bob Dylan to do a concert.'
The messages conveyed by Geldof and others, in Bruce's
words, 'sowed the seed', and, over time, Bruce got involved
as a volunteer campaigner for Oxfam, where his growing
awareness of the harsh facts of international poverty fostered
a deepening determination that something had to change. 'I
went to an Oxfam workshop where I discovered that a child is
dying every three seconds from poverty. I learnt that we take
more from continents like Africa in the way of debt and in
unfair trade terms than we give them in aid. I still have the
book where I discovered this. When that realisation hits home,
I say to people, "How can you not respond? How can you
possibly go on in your life complicit with that unless you're
doing all you can to change it?"'

Many stories in this book tell of the power of personal
relationships: people who are moved to help because they have
personally seen or experienced need, because someone close
to them or people with whom they live were facing difficulty.
But it is a special kind of empathy that makes someone devote
themselves to changing the lives of people they have never met
or to fighting for the rights of communities on the other side
of the world. This is what moved me about Bruce. Our world
has got very much smaller, and the problems facing people far
away from us can no longer feel like far-away problems. Our
commitment to fighting their injustices must be as urgent and
immediate as our commitment to fighting our own. For Bruce,
global trade is not just a news item any more: it is personal.

Determined to find practical ways to fight the injustices they
were learning about, Bruce and the Garstang Oxfam Group
turned their focus to the issue of Fairtrade. The Fairtrade
mark means that consumers can be sure when they purchase
products that disadvantaged producers in the developing world
are getting a fair deal. There is a guarantee that commodities
are produced in accordance with labour, environmental and
social standards, and a fair price covers not only the cost of

sustainable production but additionally an amount is invested in social or economic development projects. 'We were a group that campaigned on lots of issues, but Fairtrade was something that was a particular favourite of ours. It is a message that people understand very well and know what action they can take. Many times in the past people have done things – they've gone on marches, they've submitted petitions to government – but it doesn't change anything. With Fairtrade you can actually undertake action that does change something. Ultimately we want to change unfair trade rules, change the trading system: that's what this is about. But with Fairtrade, while you're working towards that, you are actually helping five million people around the world immediately.'

Despite their best efforts, Bruce and his team struggled to make progress locally, and so, feeling that people didn't have the time to listen to the many complex issues behind the campaign, the group organised a meal using Fairtrade produce and invited all the key people in the community: members of the local council, the mayor, members of the chamber of trade and local business people. 'We did not ask them to pay for the meal, and, more importantly, we didn't allow them to give donations. This is not about charity. It enabled us to get the message across, and people started asking, "Well, what is it that you want us to do?" We were simply asking for their support just to use Fairtrade products. It's very easy sometimes for people to put money into a box and buy their guilt away. Sometimes, when we realise the issues that are ahead of us regarding poverty – that we are rich because they are poor – it's very easy for people to put money into a tin and feel happier. I don't think that's the answer personally; I think people have to take some action. They have to do something to make the changes happen.'

That was the turning point in the campaign, when people began to listen. Bruce explained how he went door to door, asking each shop, each local business, to make a commitment.

The campaign succeeded: all the churches, the schools and the local council agreed to use Fairtrade products, and traders signed a pledge to use or sell Fairtrade products where possible. 'We had all these people agreeing to actually use the products, and it was then we had the idea we could create a Fairtrade community, or a Fairtrade Town; the national Fairtrade Town movement came out of that.'

At a public meeting in April 2000, the people of Garstang became the first in the world to declare themselves a Fairtrade Town. Since then, Garstang has inspired communities across the country to seek Fairtrade Town status, including members of my own constituency, and in February this year, the UK's 250th Fairtrade Town was declared. The model pioneered in this small town has now inspired similar initiatives in Sweden, Australia, Holland and Canada.

Bruce has been the leading force in efforts to spread the Fairtrade Town model across the country, but he is very reticent about accepting personal recognition for this success. He praises others in the local Oxfam Group and beyond who were involved and sees his work as just one example of work on behalf of others across Britain. 'I am not representing those people, but I am an example of those people. Nothing I'm doing is any better than what others are doing, but it's an example. This is what's being replicated all over the country.'

Despite this success, Bruce told me about how hard it can still be to get people to listen to the issues, to make people recognise the impact of their own actions and to make them realise that 'we don't have to be part of an unjust system'. He was keen to make the connections between the work to promote Fairtrade and the commemoration of the 200th anniversary of the abolition of the slave trade, citing as a hero Thomas Clarkson, the workhorse behind the abolition movement. 'Thomas Clarkson wrote an essay about the slave trade for a competition in Cambridge. He won the competition, and on his way back from getting the prize he repeatedly asked himself the question, "If what I've written is true, why is nobody doing anything about it?" This haunted him until eventually he dedicated the rest of his life to seeing an end to slavery. I can relate to that so much, because that's how I feel.

'We look back 200 years ago now to the slave trade and we think, "Oh, they must have been evil people, these people who were trading." They weren't. They were just like we are today. I think in 200 years' time, people will look back at us and say, "They must have been so evil and ignorant about what they were doing to their world. They were sitting back and eating their chocolate whilst people growing the cocoa didn't even have access to clean water and were dying from lack of healthcare. How could they live like that?" My question is like Thomas Clarkson's, "Why is everybody not doing something about this? Why are we all not doing far more than just buying Fairtrade products?" What I try to do is make people wake up to that realisation the same way that I did. Really, there isn't a choice: that's the thing I've begun to realise more recently. When you have that feeling, when you know what's happening in the world and you know that it's wrong, I don't believe there is a choice.'

Bruce continues to work part time as a vet and now works with the Fairtrade Foundation, passionately spreading the word about what each of us can do. His work in Garstang continues, with plans this summer to encourage the town to renew its pledges. Alongside the Fairtrade Town campaign, he works with the town's youth on a project aimed at building long-term partnerships with students and farmers in Ghana, which has included a youth trip to Ghana, and he is now developing the town's partnership with the cocoa-producing community of New Koforidua.

'The high points are talking to producers, talking to the beneficiaries: to be able to shake their hand, look them in the eye, and to hear from their lips that what I'm doing is right. I can take the frustration that comes from dealing with local councils. I can take the frustration of hearing absurd comments from the general public, like: "They're poor because they're lazy", and even the frustration of seeing what governments are doing. I can take it when I hear the producers saying, "Please carry on what you're doing. What you're doing is right and you're doing it for us and we want you to carry on." That's the high point, without a doubt.'

MENTORS

There is a story told of a drug dealer asked by an American church minister, 'Why did we lose you? Why are we losing other kids now?' The drug dealer replied, 'I'm there, you're not. When the kids go to school, I'm there, you're not. When the boy goes out for a loaf of bread, I'm there, you're not. When he wants someone older to talk to or feel safe and strong around, I'm there, you're not . . .'

Being there – human beings being human, listening, comforting, supporting, mentoring – is the first line of support for the individual in need. 'It is not only possible for one human being to make a real and lasting difference to another,' writes David Robinson, co-founder of Community Links and of We Are What We Do, 'it is often the only thing that ever does. No matter how rich or poor, whatever our faith or ethnicity, it is others who feed and comfort us when we are young, teach and guide us as we grow, restore our spirits when we're bereaved. Corporations can't, computers can't, officialdom can't. Only people can.'

In this section, I tell the stories of the one-to-one relationships that are transforming lives: the eighty-four-year-old athletics coach training our future Olympians, and the twenty-one-year-old volunteer helping to ensure others receive the legal advice which helped him turn his own life around; the women providing vital support to those who have experienced domestic violence and to victims of trafficking; the coaches using football to tackle racism; the firefighter using the fire service to engage disaffected young people, and the mentor supporting a refugee to build a new home; the mother who passed her dedication to caring on to her daughter, and the wife who set up a friendship group to provide support for her husband; the gardener who runs allotments at which asylum seekers can find a little peace, and the man so troubled by the hopelessness that drove his best friend to suicide that he has devoted his life to bringing hope to others and helped a thousand people into employment in the process.

These are stories of the power of the human touch, and across the country, in every sector and setting, I have seen the power of one-to-one relationships to make a difference to people's lives and help them to solve their own problems. In fact, all our great challenges – drug rehabilitation, teenage vandalism and young offenders, troubled children in and coming out of care, the adult unemployed, the lonely pensioner – have one thing in common: that they need and can benefit from one-to-one care, attention and mentoring, one-to-one care that markets and governments have never been the best at delivering. And these challenges can be fully addressed only through the choices people make to engage personally in our shared desire for a better society.

One-to-one approaches are working in new ways and in new areas, with encouraging results. While I was writing this book, I visited Birmingham, where I met the chief constable and local police chiefs involved in tackling gang, gun and drugs crime. What became clear to me is that the one-to-one approach can be highly effective in dealing with potential and actual criminals. After a spate of murders, the police had arrested and imprisoned leaders of local gangs but then found they had to deal with younger members now taking over. So alongside arrests and imprisonments, they also worked on conflict mediation to prevent a new outbreak of violence between the gangs. That in turn led on to them doing one-to-one mentoring and coaching: helping young individuals out of gangs and, for the first time, into ordered lives, structured around jobs as well as homes. And they also found that by directly warning each father – often an absent father – that their teenage son's life was at risk in gangs, they enlisted the absentee dad back as a figure of authority working to change that son's life. Today, the results of this one-to-one approach are being felt across the community: the father of a young gun victim who died is now working to encourage his son's friends to break with the gangs, and one former gang member is one of the leaders of the local campaign calling for Birmingham's young people to leave behind guns and gangs.

Today, mentoring is also being used as a means of early intervention to ensure that young people are given the individual support that will enable them to fulfil their potential. The range of approaches include organisations such as Chance UK, which pairs mentors with children aged five to eleven judged at risk of drifting into criminal behaviour as they approach their teens, or Parents as First Teachers, which works one-to-one with parents of young children to support and nurture their parenting skills and confidence in raising their children.

Schools too provide vital opportunities to realise the power of one-to-one. We all remember the one teacher who shaped our lives, who took the time to really get to know us and to inspire us as individuals. And in addition to the vital work of all our teachers, one-to-one tutoring initiatives such as Every Child a Reader and the planned Every Child Counts are demonstrating how much can be achieved when children receive dedicated, personalised support. But it is not only teachers who are employing this approach; pupils are too, with schools across the country running peer-to-peer mentoring schemes in which pupils are trained to act as mentors to other pupils who are looking for personal or academic support.

Buddying and befriending schemes are supporting individuals and families affected by a range of disabilities and medical conditions, with particularly innovative work being undertaken to support those affected by HIV/Aids. And countless local visiting schemes are pairing volunteers with elderly members of their local communities to help them to overcome their isolation and to maintain their independence and mental well-being.

The power of a one-to-one approach is that it can be a way of reaching out to and providing support for people who are often hard to engage and help adequately via conventional approaches – including some particularly vulnerable or at-risk groups, such as the homeless, refugees, the long-term unemployed, looked-after children, those with mental-health difficulties, offenders and ex-offenders. For example, schemes developed by organisations such as Rainer and CSV are pairing volunteers with children in care to offer friendship to those who may have no special adult in their life who can spend time with them individually. Innovative mentoring schemes developed by organisations such as the Prince's Trust not only provide vital support to ex-offenders but also encourage ex-offenders to become mentors themselves to young people who have become involved in crime. And TimeBank's range of successful mentoring initiatives include matching more than 2,500 refugees with mentors all over the country and a scheme matching men who have experienced mental illness and are looking to build their personal, professional and social skills back up with a male mentor of a similar age.

Online or telephone counselling and mentoring offer opportunities to give and receive personal support in a convenient and anonymous way – from the essential support offered by helplines such as the Samaritans and Childline to innovative web-mentoring such as horsesmouth, which encourages people to share their experiences with others who might benefit from them.

And of course, many of the most important one-to-one relationships take place not through any formal structure or organisation but through the many, many informal relation-ships through which we care for, support and encourage our families and our friends. Those who care for their elderly parents as well as their young children; those who foster or adopt as well as those who raise their own children; those who support a loved one through an illness or disability; those who are a friend and a neighbour, who are there in good times and bad.

As Albert Schweitzer said: 'In everyone's life, at some time, our inner fire goes out. It is then burst into flame by an encounter with another human being. We should all be thankful for those people who rekindle the inner spirit.'

The power of the human touch is, I believe, driven by more than enlightened self-interest. Call it, as Adam Smith did, the 'moral sentiment'; or Winstanley, 'the light in man'; or Beveridge, 'the driving power of social conscience'. Is it not a moral sense – a moral impulse that moves and motivates us all – that can inspire us to anger at injustice and at inhumanity when it blights the lives of others even in the most remote and harshest corner of the earth?

The moral impulse may not be 'the strong beacon of light' that we would like it to be, but often, in the words of Professor James Q. Wilson, 'a small candle flame, casting vague and multiple shadows, flickering and sputtering in the strong winds of power and passion, greed and ideology', but, as he writes, 'brought close to the heart and cupped in one's hands, it dispels the darkness and warms the soul'. Each of my inspirations in this book reminded me of that candle, in both their frailty and their power. As Sheffield football coach Kevin Titterton said, 'You can only do a bit, can't you? It may seem at times, as it has to me when I've been down, like a drop in the ocean, but if you can do your bit to make communities better, it's just better for us all.'

For the child in care, the young family stretched to breaking point, the elderly neighbour entirely alone, strength and hope and friendship come not from markets and states, or incentives and commands, but from the human touch. From teachers and mentors, from the dedicated volunteer or the committed carer or the good neighbour, one-to-one, day after day, with each 'doing their bit' or just 'being there'. It is a gift that, as these stories show, changes lives. And my conclusion is that we have a duty as a government to do more to sponsor, finance and support the great people whose one-to-one work takes patience, time and effort and needs to be properly resourced as well as fully recognised.

8

JILL PAY AND CAMILLA McCREADY PAY

You can change things for yourself and you can change things for others: this is the one-to-one stuff that you can't put a price on.

Jill Pay was kind enough to invite me to her home in Camden, north London, where I met her and two of her three children, her daughters Camilla, twenty, and Rowan, eighteen, and came face to face with the everyday challenges facing Britain's six million carers.

When Rowan was born, she had birth asphyxia and wasn't expected to survive. But cared for in the Special Care Baby Unit at University College Hospital she came through. Rowan is now eighteen and has very severe learning difficulties and needs twenty-four-hour care. Her wonderful smile hides her low communication skills, limited mobility and severe disability. Although it was not apparent, she also suffers from epilepsy and scoliosis. Rowan loves music, and she likes being spoken to, even though she cannot respond.

When Rowan was born, Jill had three children under five. 'In those early days, we were thrown in the deep end. My life was twenty-four-hour caring, which it normally is with a new baby. Of course, I'd had children before, so I knew about babies, but it wasn't the same. There was the constant fear that she could die at any moment. Plus there was the impact on the family. Camilla was just two, Alex was just four, and

73

they had to be taken care of by friends and family, some closer than others. So, they were quite often kind of farmed out at very short notice. Rowan suffered from a failure to thrive several times during the first year of her life and had to be taken into hospital. There was a very heightened state of anxiety the whole time: it was full on, and I hardly got any sleep.'

After several years of juggling informal support from friends and family, and fighting hard for what little professional support was available to carers at that time, Jill managed to find a specialist nursery to care for Rowan. 'It was Rainbow House Day Nursery in Pimlico; I secured a place there for her three mornings a week. But I had to arrange all the transportation. So, at that point I spent my days taking Alex to school, Camilla to nursery and Rowan to Pimlico: running round all the different places. I'd do the morning run and then I'd go home, and then it was more or less time to turn round and go and do the reverse journey. I spent my whole time running round until Rowan's nursery intervened and contacted our social worker, saying, "This woman is exhausted. You cannot let her keep doing this."'

Rowan attended the nursery for about three years and then started at the Jack Taylor School, a specialist severe-learning-difficulties school where she has been ever since. Rowan has always loved going to school, where she is well cared for, and now Jill has some breaks, some of which are provided by Camden Crossroads.

Jill ensured that each of her children was given the care and support they needed. 'I think it's fair to say I always tried to make sure that Alex and Camilla had as normal a life as possible in terms of engaging with local activities. But I believe that a young disabled person or child should just join in with everyday life; they shouldn't be excluded. So wherever we went, Rowan went, and she just joined the fairly close community that we were part of. We attended all the events for the kids in the local park, and we took part in everything that was going on – all together.'

After Rowan began school, Jill didn't confine her role to providing the care and support needed by her own family; she joined with others to provide a support network and to campaign for improved services for other carers. 'I came across the Camden Parents' Forum: now that's come and gone. But at the time it was a group of parents of disabled children who used to meet together monthly as a sort of support group. But we also campaigned, and we campaigned quite vigorously. We identified areas that were of particular interest to each of us. So, at the time mine was housing, while for others it might have been education or health. And we structured our campaigning so that we weren't all just taking on the whole lot.

'We developed a thing called "Every Day Is Day One". When you were telling your story to a professional, a social worker or whoever it was, you always had to go through the whole story every single time and it was like starting all over again. We asked why there couldn't be some kind of centralised information system or a way of doing it so that the basics didn't have to keep being re-told. Out of that campaign, local social services responded by setting up the Disabled Children's Team, which was dedicated to supporting families with disabled children. I think it's important to make the point that if you state your case clearly and strongly enough, you can influence policy and make changes.

'The whole time I've been caring and dealing with social services or any other professionals, I've always been aware that I have a very strong voice. I can articulate and say what I mean, but there are, behind me, a hell of a lot of people who do not have that voice and don't even know where to start to go. There are a lot of hidden carers. There are a lot of people who just don't even know that they can ask for things.'

Jill is one of six million loved and loving carers of those close to them, carers who are the very heart of our compassionate society and an immense force for good. Her trials and struggles, like millions of others, often go without recognition, not acknowledged and appreciated as they should be. Every week, almost 40,000 people become carers for the first time, often with little warning or preparation. In two decades, the number of carers could rise to nine million, and at some point in their lives 70 per cent of women and 60 per cent of men will act as carers. 'When you look at the statistics, the contribution that carers actually make in pure money terms, in Camden alone it's something like £175 million. If every carer pulled out, that's what would have to be found. Although I don't want to look at it in those terms, that's the value, that's what it represents. Nationally, it's the equivalent of a second NHS. It's huge. More people are going to become carers, even if it's only later in life for a short term. That's no less of a caring role. You may have to give up work because there's no other way round it.'

It's a family business. Jill's older daughter Camilla has also been involved in caring for her sister over the years and is determined to make a career of it. For Camilla, having a little sister with special needs was just part of growing up, but it wasn't always easy. 'We did have some difficult times with each other when I was very little. I didn't understand, I suppose. I used to get very upset when she was unwell. I always used to be late for school because we'd have to wait for her bus to come before Mum could take me. So, until I was independent enough to go on my own, I was always late for school. But I've always helped Mum look after Rowan, because I didn't like looking at my mum doing it all.'

When Rowan was twelve and Camilla fourteen, they started attending an arts-based youth group: WAC Performing Arts and Media College. Camilla initially went along as a volunteer to support her sister. 'Really, in the early days, I was joining in and having fun, but the role developed, and I ended up going away with them on a residential course and actually taking care of young people with an older member of staff watching me. When I was eighteen, I got a job in a special-needs school. I still work there as a teaching assistant, and I continue to do volunteering work in other forms. I still have contact with some of the young people that have left the school. I often take them out in the holidays, and there's one particular young man that I see every week. I take him swimming, to the cinema: stuff like that, just one-to-one. I'm still doing some paid work at WAC, and though there are times when they don't have the money to pay people, I still go along and do the work.'

Although Camilla is now studying for a degree in youth and community work, she continues to support others. 'Over Easter, I took two young people to the beach, and it was amazing to see them. They were away from their parents and from a regimented school environment . . . they were free. This young man, he's in a wheelchair, and he's never wanted to get out of his wheelchair, but as soon as he saw the beach, he said, "I want to get out." Just seeing that happiness, that's what motivates me. That's why I do it.'

Jill is so committed to caring that she is also a volunteer, helping other carers and training social workers in the techniques of care. 'One of the things I do with care managers and social workers is an exercise where they have to identify a time in their own lives when they were caring and when they were cared for. We actually explore the emotional issues around that. It's a very powerful exercise, and it gets them starting to think in a different way about what caring really means. Most of them, actually, come up with something from both sides, and, even if it's only temporary, they can begin to get a feel for what it might be like. It's about breaking down a lot of preconceived ideas around the role of carer.'

Jill also provides training for carers: looking at the skills they acquire during the course of their caring that might help them get work or go on training courses at a later date. She is passionate about the importance of ensuring that carers' skills are recognised and about the status of carers. She also feels that it is vital that carers have opportunities to combine work and care.

'Carers really need to be recognised and seen in a positive light. When you've been caring for a long time, whether that's as a parent carer or whatever, and suddenly you're looking to move out of your caring role, there are a lot of difficulties around getting back into the workplace, some of which are quite well hidden. I want carers themselves to identify and acknowledge the skills and strategies that we've learnt just by being in the role. I run a course called "All About Me for a Change". One of the first things we do is a big brainstorm where we ask, "OK, what do you do?" They list things like nurse, advocate, specialist cook and negotiator. There are huge, huge amounts of skills actually involved, and by the time we've finished that exercise, everyone's sitting up proudly realising their own worth.

'You see that you can get results. The last carers' course that I ran was just so amazing: the connections that people made and the real moves they made in their lives. You can change things for yourself and you can change things for others: this is the one-to-one stuff that you can't put a price on.'

Jill displays enormous energy and compassion, and her selflessness and concern for others is moving. 'I sometimes look at my situation and think, "I'm having a walk in the park compared with some people." You hear their stories and what they have to contend with every day and you think, "Blimey!"'

For Jill and Camilla, caring is not just a profession, it is far more a matter of love than of duty: caring that expresses itself in the priceless gift of sustained and dedicated support for people close to them. They are just one family amongst so many who, when faced with challenges, respond with unconditional love and care. And they are an inspiration.

9

DAVE GREEN

I took up coaching because I love the sport and I wanted to give something back to the club . . . Over the years, I do not know how many youngsters I have coached. It must be something like 2,000 . . . We have had a lot of champions during that time.

In the east London borough of Newham, preparations are underway for the 2012 Olympics. Construction is beginning on the sites that will house the sporting events, and as local residents begin to see their neighbourhood changing, excitement has started to grow. The prospect of competing in the Olympics has fired the imagination of many young athletes, who dream of running in their home city. Schools are seeing more of their pupils signing up to participate in Olympic sports, and at the local athletics club, Newham and Essex Beagles, many of these young people are being coached by eighty-four-year-old Dave Green.

It's amazing that someone who was born in time for the 1924 Olympics in Paris is now coaching athletes for the 2012 Olympics in London. But Dave has been coaching young people at the same club for more than fifty years. The walking stick he uses following a hip operation hasn't slowed Dave down at all, and he can still be found at the club twice a week, running training sessions for aspiring athletes.

With a modesty that suggested Dave saw nothing particularly remarkable in the length and extent of his commitment to his club, he explained how it all began. 'I joined the club in

1946 and started coaching in 1951. Our club was based then at Dagenham in Essex. We moved when we needed an all-weather track, and we have been here since 1983. I have done sixty-one years since I joined the club, but I am just completing fifty-six years of coaching. I think I have done every job in this club, from chairman to secretary to treasurer. I only gave up the treasurer-ship last year.'

Dave has had a keen interest in athletics since his schooldays, which saw him compete in the All England Schools' Championships. Having left school at fourteen to go out to work, he served in the RAF during the Second World War, and in 1945 returned to civilian life. 'When I came out of the RAF, I went back to my old firm, and it just so happened that the new accountant manager heard of my interest in athletics. He lived next door to the treasurer of Newham and Essex Beagles, or Essex Beagles as it was called then. That was my introduction to the club, which was in 1946.

'I was only a moderate athlete myself. But after about five years I suffered an injury that really put paid to my athletics career. One of the coaches suggested I take up coaching, and that is what I did. At that time, I was coaching triple jump, and then I went on to do some long-jump training as well. I finished up doing middle-distance training, and I have been doing that ever since, probably since 1955, I should think. I took up coaching because I love the sport and I wanted to give something back to the club in the first instance. I went through the exams and the coaching, and I am level four now, which is the top one before you become an international coach. Over the years, I do not know how many youngsters I have coached. It must be something like 2,000 of all ages from eleven to nineteen. We have had lots of champions during that time.'

Dave spoke about how much he enjoys what he does and how much he still gets out of it. 'I have a bunch of under-thirteens at the moment. I suppose there's about thirteen or fourteen of them, and I get a lot of respect. Whatever they get from me, I get a lot from them as well, because, at eighty-four, it keeps you a little bit young, keeps your mind active. I enjoy it very much, and if you enjoy what you are doing, it does not become work. The squad I have got now vary quite considerably in their athletic skills, but they are a great bunch. They are very friendly, and they help one another. It builds good team spirit and a good feeling for the youngsters. I feel they do me good, and I hope I am doing them some good.'

After sticking with the same club for so many years, Dave has seen generations of young athletes come and go, but the care and effort he puts into coaching stays with them. Many still remember Dave and keep in touch, and, chatting with him, it's easy to understand why. 'Some of the athletes I coached twenty or thirty years ago are now in their forties. You meet them now and again. I can't remember who they are, but they always remember who I am. It is very embarrassing sometimes. When I was walking down the High Street one day, a young man came up to me and said, "Are you Dave Green?" I said, "Yes, I am, but I'm sorry, I don't know who you are", and he said, "You used to coach me when I was fourteen." He is forty-five now, and we've become great friends again. He comes round every Friday for a cup of tea.

'I trained a man called Graeme Fell who went to Canada and became Commonwealth champion. He came back over recently after his mother died. He found out where I lived and came round, and we had a chat together for about an hour and a half.'

While it has been, first and foremost, Dave's love for his sport that has motivated him over the years, he has also seen the impact that sport can have on young people's lives. He hasn't tried to be their youth worker or their counsellor or their mentor; he has just been their coach, but his impact can be felt far beyond the track. 'I think sport makes a big difference to the youngsters. I think it strengthens their characters: well, it does if you treat them correctly. I treat them as adults. They could see my point of view, and I could see their point of view. If they want to say something, then you listen to them. It is not me as a coach telling them what to do all the time. In this particular area, there are a lot of very unfortunate children. A lot of things happen around here, but you do not get any problems once they come into sport. We have had youngsters over here who have been in trouble, but it has worked out once you get them really interested. A lot of them are good kids anyway right from the start. The kids that come on their own are the ones that really need to be looked after more, because they have no encouragement from their families or anybody else. We have been trying to develop a relationship with their parents. The kids are all very keen, and the more input you give to them the keener they get.'

His years at the club have left Dave with many memories, and a few club members in particular stand out as inspirations to him. 'We had Daley Thompson at our club as a young boy: a bit of a rebel. I never coached him, but one of my friends did, and he was an inspiration to me because he was a fantastic athlete. But I also remember there were three boys that I used to pick up on the way, three lads from an ordinary family of seven boys and four girls. They had no transport; the father and mother were quite ordinary people, like me. It was really inspiring to hear about those three boys: now one of them is a professor in Scotland, one has a senior job in the Health Service, and the other one is . . . bird watching in Wales, I think was what I heard! But these are the kind of people that inspire you.'

But along with the inspirations there have been disappointments, particularly because Dave is so keen to spot talent and to see potential in those not always able to see it in themselves. 'You have to be the right sort of person to be able to take it all, because you have to take disappointments as well. Kids come and they really show good promise but do not stay. You see a champion disappearing. It is quite disappointing at times.'

While Dave continues to give his time each week, both to

coaching young athletes and to training a new generation of volunteer coaches, finding those willing to take up his mantle is proving very difficult. And while neither boisterous teenagers nor a hip operation have ever tempted him to give up, the lack of enough fellow willing volunteers nearly did. 'It is very difficult to get the volunteers to do the work now: it's the time factor, I suppose. People are working, but we have got a number of coaches here who give up their time. I mean, it is very easy for me because I am retired. This year I was almost tempted to give up, but since the Olympics was awarded here things have really come to life. All the schools have nominated their best young athletes or people they think might progress to the Olympics, and several of mine are in that squad.'

As he looks forward to the Olympics in 2012, Dave is full of hope for what his young athletes might achieve. His loyalty, his energy and his good humour mean that, while the next few years will bring much change to this area and its sports clubs, Dave's place at the very heart of this community looks secure. 'I have always lived well away from the track. It is a twenty-mile journey there and back. But I am one of those kinds of people who, if you join a club, then I like to stay with the same club. I could easily change to another club that is nearer, but once you get involved with a club, you stay with it. I could not let the club down, really, and that is what it boils down to. There's no way that I could have let them go, and I think I shall be doing this until I drop.'

When we think about the people who are changing our society for the better, we often rightly celebrate the innovators, the pioneers and the activists always searching for the next new way to make a difference. But in this book, I also wanted to tell the stories of a very different sort of volunteer: those people who find a need and quietly give their time, those people who keep on giving their time without ever seeking recognition. Those people who find a way to do something good and then just keep on doing it: in Dave's case, for fifty-six years and counting.

10

COLIN ZETIE

Every day, someone's life is changing just because you've had an idea and you've put it down on the back of a fag packet and made it happen.

Colin Zetie's story is a compelling illustration of how by changing your life you can turn adversity into a powerful force for good. Today, Colin is head of employment initiatives with Groundwork East London. Groundwork is a national environmental regeneration charity working in partnership with local people, local authorities and business to promote economic and social regeneration in communities in need of investment.

Colin is an inspiring and highly successful professional who has personally helped more than a thousand people return to sustainable employment. But, as he knows so well, his life could have turned out very differently. 'I was brought up in Birmingham and ended up living in the most densely populated two square miles of northern Europe, a place called Castle Vale. I wasn't too clever. I'm an ex-offender, and I struggled to get into a normal job for about ten years until my record was spent. It's hard. I've done stuff like gardening, I was a grave digger for a couple of years, and I've been a road sweeper, just anything.' These experiences have motivated Colin to dedicate the past ten years of his life to helping people find employment and find new purpose in their lives.

Colin told me about his hopelessness as a young man, the

belief that he had no prospects or opportunities, which led him to leave school at sixteen and spend the next few years getting into trouble with the law. But two events were turning points for Colin, the moments when he knew he had to make a change for the better. First, his best friend committed suicide aged twenty-one. I asked Colin why his friend had done it, and the tone of his reply spoke volumes about the shared hopelessness that dominated Colin's early life and environment. 'He lived on the sixteenth floor of a tower block. He had no job and no chance of ever getting a job. He had no hope, no chance of things ever changing.' This tragedy, and others that affected Colin's peers, were the beginnings of a wake-up call. 'You just thought, "This is really hopeless."' And then shortly after that came a second, critical turning point: Colin had a child. 'And then I knew I really needed to sort my life out.' Now a father of two, with a grandchild on the way, Colin recognises the importance of these personal experiences. 'Everyone's got a bit of history here at Groundwork, and I think there's a personal reason why everyone's in this work. I think back to where I was, and I'm trying to do this so it helps people who are in the same situation that I was. And my experiences help in my work, because people look at me, see my tattoos, and they can tell I'm the same as them.'

Long-term unemployment can have devastating con-sequences not just for the individuals involved but also for the prospects, aspirations and cohesion of their families and communities. When we are able to support someone back into work, the positive ripple effects can be endless. And that is why those who are working to achieve this, be they in the public, private or voluntary sector, are so vital: they are not simply offering training and skills; they are offering hope to whole communities.

Groundwork East London initiates local projects around four themes – health, education, the environment and public safety – and uses the project opportunities to provide work-related training and experience. 'I work mainly with people who we now call "workless". We target the most disadvantaged areas where few other people go. We are working with lone parents, people with disabilities, those for whom English is a second language: people who cannot take part in mainstream unemployment schemes offered by the Government.'

As Colin proudly explained, Groundwork's programmes have achieved very impressive results. 'One of our education programmes trains lone parents to work in local schools. At the moment, one in five people working in schools in Hackney have come through our programmes. A lot of them move on into special educational needs work, and we get about one in ten who actually goes on to teach, which is quite good when you think that a few years ago these people were on benefits. We did a programme recently with the local hospital where we trained people to do the administrative roles in the hospital, and twenty-eight out of the thirty got jobs there.'

But while Groundwork's primary focus is on training and employment, evidence of its impact can be felt across the local community in terms of community cohesion, improved local services and community engagement.

'We run a "green team", where we do elderly and disabled people's gardens. It bridges that generation gap. We're supporting the old guys down the allotments and do all the hard grunt work for them. There was some land that was derelict when we first got it. We got guys with some quite serious learning difficulties to clear the land, we laid it out with donations from the Chelsea Flower Show, and now there are three football pitches. About 150 kids play football there every weekend, and from being somewhere where even the police just didn't want to go it's turned into a place that the community can use. And then there's a public safety project, where we're engaging different communities to get them to become Police Community Support Officers. We're digging into minority groups so the police will be more representative.'

Much of Groundwork's success lies in its focus not simply on developing core work-related skills but on the wider personal development of each of the individuals they work with. And with each of the many stories Colin was eager to tell, he showed just how wide reaching the impacts of this approach could be. 'We often work with people who have got quite a few issues at first. One young man had such problems he couldn't even dress himself in the morning. If his brother didn't dress him with a coat, he'd just arrive, even in the winter, wearing a T-shirt and thin trousers. All the other guys took responsibility for him, and they'd bring clothes in and dress him. Even though at first they were complaining about him, it made them all grow up. He eventually got a job working as a gardener for a church, which, for that guy, it's incredible.

'There was another young guy who had been out of work since he left school. We got him a job working in the HR department at Homerton Hospital. You could see he just hadn't looked after himself, but after about six months there, he's got a bigger build, he's obviously got a better diet, he's going to the gym. It's like seeing a different person altogether. It wasn't just the fact that he had a job and a couple of quid, but everything was just different. His confidence levels had increased, and he'd look you in the eye.'

What was so apparent when listening to Colin talk about his work is that for him and his team every individual counts: not as a target or a box to be ticked but as an individual with a personal story and personal challenges, and with unique potential to draw out. And that's why, when you ask him about his work, he chooses to tell you story after story of individual lives transformed. 'Everyone develops personal relationships here. The staff get to understand the circumstances and conditions of the people they're working with; they know everyone's name, their kids' names, their partners' names. You generate a level of trust, especially with people who've been quite difficult with you to start with, and you break down those barriers. The best thing we ever had was someone sending their mum to us to help her get a job. That is trust when someone sends you their mum!'

Central to building this trust is Groundwork's commitment to practising what they preach. 'Around 20 per cent of the Groundwork staff have come through our training programmes. We've probably got three or four lone mums working for us because we'll be really flexible about their hours.'

What is striking about Colin is not just his dedication to his work but his absolute love for what he does. 'It's just absolutely brilliant doing it. It is such a buzz. You couldn't get a job that you get as much joy out of. It's a funny feeling when you get up, get dressed to go to work in the morning, and you think to yourself, probably two people a week in Hackney get jobs because of what happens here. Two people a week get jobs in Newham because of what happens there, and it's getting like that in Waltham Forest. Every day, someone's life is changing just because you've had an idea and you've put it down on the back of a fag packet and made it happen.'

Eager not to be marked out as a 'hero', Colin is full of praise for all those engaged in this vital work. 'My team are inspirational to me, all different personalities, and I think, "You lot are just really putting it in. No matter what, you put it in." There are people from local authorities who go that extra mile all the time. There are people in certain government departments who take a little bit of a risk with us and stuff like that. People who really mean what they are doing. I think, "You're in a nice safe world, and you could just live in the don't-rock-the-boat world and be really comfortable", but they put in the work. You can see that sort of commitment, and you think, "Yeah, these are just good people." Year in, year out, I look at my team and see how dedicated and committed they are, and I think, "These guys don't deserve to be on year-on-year contracts." I know how hard they work, especially when there's a certain ethos. Everyone believes in what they're doing.'

Colin and his stories filled me with optimism. He and his team, day after day, are achieving victories of the human spirit that are translating into huge changes for the individuals they work with, their families and their communities. Getting someone back into sustainable employment isn't just about skills, it is about the care and patience that can give someone the self-belief and the aspirations to turn their life around. One story in particular struck me as testimony to Colin's unique blend of compassion and down-to-earth determination. 'One guy I remember, no one wanted to touch. He'd done ten years inside for being involved in a bank raid. His mates tried to give themselves up, so he started shooting them, and the police, obviously, were quite cross about it. I ended up bringing him onto a training programme, and everyone said, "No, he's really dangerous." I had a chat with him and took him on; I kept him away from my staff. I thought, "If he's going to be a handful, I'll deal with him myself." But he was perfect on the programme: the guy passed his driving test, passed all the training, so we gave him a waged opportunity and then a permanent job. He worked for me for two years, never a day off sick, brilliant with the lads. A couple of years later, he moved on to work for one of our partner companies, and I got a message saying, "Thanks a lot. I couldn't even steal the amount of money I'm earning at the moment." He's got a house. He's settled down. It's just like really perfect, and he's such a really nice guy. It's just a buzz when you hear that, you get a smile on your face.'

11

KEVIN TITTERTON AND DESBON BUSHIRI RUBAMBA

Everyone says it's not like it used to be, there's no community spirit any more, but they don't do anything about it. If you get involved, you can change something.

You might expect Kevin Titterton and Desbon Bushiri Rubamba to be worlds apart. Kevin was born and brought up in Sheffield and describes himself as 'basically a white working-class lad'. Desbon is a young man who, at age eighteen, arrived alone in the UK from Burundi, seeking asylum. But these men, with their different life stories, have a shared passion: football. Kevin as a spectator and lifelong Sheffield United supporter, and Desbon as a skilful player and talented coach. Their unlikely connection is just one of the inspiring stories to come out of the Football Unites, Racism Divides (FURD) community campaign in Sheffield.

As we see during international tournaments, football can provide a focus that brings together people from different backgrounds to play, watch and enjoy the game. The world's most popular sport has an amazing ability to break down barriers created by ignorance or prejudice. But sadly, far from uniting, football can itself also become a focus for racism, as Kevin explained. 'My involvement in FURD stretches back to virtually the beginning. There used to be a Sheffield United fans organisation called Blades Independent Fans Association, and at the 1996 AGM I spoke about racism in football. A lot of us Sheffield United fans had concerns about problems that were occurring on match day around the ground. Our football ground, which we go to at least once a fortnight, this hallowed area that we go to like a shrine, is in the middle of an area where there's a lot of Asian people and black people, yet they never came to a match. That community, Sharrow, incorporates the home of the Blades, and it's where I spent the early part of my life. I got talking to different people that live round there and found they were almost under siege on match days. They either went out for the day or they locked their doors. I thought, "This isn't right." The local people, Asian and black residents, lived in fear, and something had to change. Through Football Unites, there was an opportunity to join something as a volunteer and try to redress the situation, which obviously I was up for.'

It wasn't long before Kevin's commitment to tackling racism in his home community was put to practical use. He designed and built the original Streetkick: a wooden-panelled transportable football pitch. Streetkick has now developed into one of FURD's most high-profile areas of work. The idea is to travel to a location in a park or in a shopping precinct, set up the Streetkick pitch and invite young people to come and play football in small tournaments.

Kevin enthusiastically explained the impact that this simple idea has had. 'It's such a great platform for getting any message across. Over the years we have done not just anti-racism but sportsmanship and anti-drugs messages, we've covered all sorts of issues. Streetkick attracts the interest, and we have goody bags with football magazines, *Match of the Day* stuff, all these little bits in there: the kids love that sort of stuff. We also included anti-drugs information for young people: if you hand ten out and one person reads it, then it's getting a good message across. You can go into schools, police offices and fire stations, anywhere, and talk about things. First of all you grab the attention of the kids who participate in something they enjoy, then you hand out stuff. You are involving young people. We say, "Look, we want you to learn about this, but you come in and be involved in learning; it's not just us teaching you."'

The original wooden version of Streetkick has been replaced by an ultra-modern and larger inflatable pitch that has toured internationally and was even used during the 2006 World Cup in Germany. And Kevin's passion for the project has grown, too. 'The reason my involvement is so strong is because it's just a brilliant project for doing community work. Everyone moans about their communities, we all do it: crime, young people, whatever. You can only do a bit, can't you? It may seem at times, as it has to me when I've been a bit down, like a drop in the ocean, but if you can do your bit to make communities better, it's just better for us all, isn't it?'

Desbon Bushiri Rubamba came to this country aged eighteen as an asylum seeker in July 2000. 'I found a flat close to Sheffield United's stadium. I was a former footballer, but I didn't know anybody here in Sheffield, so I went to play football and found a game going on in the local park. I met a coach from Football Unites, who was a refugee himself, and he explained they do things like mobile football, coaching young people in different places in the community. I asked him if I could join them so I could do my football. The guy saw that I was a good player, and they invited me to go to the project: that's how I got involved.'

Desbon signed up as a Millennium Volunteer and did more than 200 hours of volunteer work as a youth coach. 'That's when everything kicked off for me. I went for trials with Sheffield United, and then I played for the reserves, scoring on my debut against Bury, but I didn't make it to a professional contract at Sheffield United. I was very disappointed, but I signed to play for Matlock Town in the Unibond First Division.'

Desbon is now a paid worker with FURD: a community football coach on the Positive Futures project, working with young people at risk of involvement with the criminal justice system by engaging them in sport. 'I'm coaching, working with young people and trying to support and guide them. I organise events in Sheffield and coordinate support and guidance for young people. We coach them in sport, and we also give them confidence to say, "I'm going to be a better person."'

I found Desbon's story particularly moving, because in helping so many young people to make changes in their lives, he has been able to build a new life for himself; in helping others participate in their communities, he has found his own community. 'My country, Burundi, had been in a state of civil war since '93. I came here when I was eighteen. I was very young. All the conflict led me to flee the country and then to come here. When I arrived, I didn't know anybody: no colleagues, no family, not anything. I wanted to become part of the community. It's an honour and a privilege to be in this country. I've got a family, I have a wife and we have a child. This is where I belong now. We all appreciate this country because of the support from local people. I have already applied for citizenship and I'm waiting to hear, but I will do anything I can in this community to help similar people in my situation or to help other people, because this is the community I now belong to.'

As Kevin added, Desbon's own story has been an important source of inspiration for him and for others involved in the project. 'You realise what people have to go through. There's this idea that everybody comes to the UK for an easy ride, and we know that's not true. We know that people come here after some real terrible situations, but he's always smiling. He's a smashing bloke, and he's great with young people: kids just respond to him. He's a brilliant footballer and a great coach. I look at people like that and I'm in awe, really.'

And while his own journey has been very different to that of Desbon, Kevin too wanted to stress the enormous benefit he has got from his involvement in community projects. 'People often say nice things about me. I do appreciate it, but I find it a bit embarrassing. The thing is, I've put a lot in, yes, but I have got tons out, I really have. I've met different kinds of people from different backgrounds, and you get to know and work with people who are really good. If you can get involved in some voluntary work, it is just brilliant. I know there's a cynical view: that you do it for yourself, for the "feel-good factor", as if there's something wrong with that. If you do voluntary work, yes, you do feel good and you're doing something positive: that is good for your soul, it's good for you as a person. You do start to make a difference, and you see that difference. All the moaning that we all do about the state of things – the gangs of youths, the state of our community – everybody moans about everything, don't they? Everyone says it's not like it used to be, there's no community spirit any more, but they don't do anything about it. If you get involved, you can change something.'

It is this commitment that drives the work of Kevin, Desbon and so many volunteers who keep on giving of their time and their energy, even when life is busy, even when it can be hard to find the time. 'I've got a wife and one son,' Kevin explained. 'They don't get as passionate, yet they've always supported me, and they've never moaned. I've been deeply involved in FURD, bank holidays are taken up with sports events and then I suddenly think, "I've not been with my family. I'm not at work, it's a bank holiday, and I should be doing something with them." But their support has always carried me through. They just say, "I wish we could see more of you, but we know you care and we understand what you're doing is a good thing", so they give me that bit of freedom.'

Football Unites runs coaching schemes for young people from across Sheffield's diverse communities and has assisted them in creating their own Sunday League teams. Young people in isolated areas of the city have been brought together to compete in leagues and tournaments, and Streetkick has been used at the heart of urban neighbourhoods to involve 'hard-to-reach' young people. As FURD demonstrates, it is often local community projects that can deliver the most powerful outcomes, and Kevin wants to make sure that the Government always remembers this. 'I know everyone asks for money, from the NHS down, but make sure that there's money available for community projects. When cutbacks have to be made and belts are tightened, try to always make sure that, right down at the bottom, community projects don't suffer. We have a diverse culture in this community, and I embrace it: I love it, me. If people don't meet and experience other people's backgrounds, they will never understand their problems: that is the thing I would say to the Government. I understand that running a country you have to have financial restraints on budgets, but the little things at the bottom mustn't be cut down.'

The work of this inspiring project continues week after week, engaging young people in something they have a passion for and, along the way, showing what we can achieve when we work together as part of a team. As Desbon said, 'We're still working, every weekend, me and all the other coaches and about a hundred kids every Sunday from different cultures, different communities and different ethnic minorities in Sheffield. We never know how those young people are going to be in the future, but we're there to help them and to support them.'

There is so much more in our common humanity that connects us with each other than separates or divides us. In our diverse society, it is inspiring to see the efforts of those working to bring us together and the friendships that are built between different people dedicated to shared goals. Football is just one example of the many shared passions that can help to build connections between neighbours and between communities. And in football teams up and down the country, the bonds of friendship and teamwork and support are being nurtured by volunteers and coaches with a passion for the game and all it can offer.

12

LALITA PATEL

This gives people a sense of security and belonging, which is a foundation that then allows them to reach out and do things together with people from other communities and cultures.

There were two major turning points in Lalita Patel's life: turning points which make her, at seventy-seven, one of Britain's inspirational carers. The first was being diagnosed with breast cancer, which in 1993 forced her to give up the business she and her husband had built in Croydon in the years since they arrived in Britain from Kenya in 1975. The second was even more traumatic, when in 1995 her husband suffered a brain haemorrhage and fell into a coma. His condition led to Lalita becoming a full-time carer and founding the Bromley Asian Cultural Association (BACA), and set her on a path where, in her seventies, she is inspiring those around her to get involved in building a stronger community.

As a result of the brain haemorrhage, Lalita's husband suffered extensive damage to the right side of his brain. It took a series of operations before he even regained consciousness. He lost access to the information stored in his brain, including his knowledge of numerous languages, and had no short-term memory. And so Lalita, like so many others, became a full-time carer, her husband completely dependent on her for his day-to-day care and support. 'He got very upset if I was away for more than half an hour,' Lalita explained. Unable to return to their house, as it had no downstairs bathroom, they went to live with one of their sons in Bromley. After a year of intensive caring, her husband recovered the ability to speak but not his short-term memory. Lalita needed to stay by his side all the time.

During this difficult period, Lalita became increasingly aware of the kind of support her husband would benefit from and the kind of support that she herself required as a carer, and she set about trying to find the help they needed. But this was no easy task. 'I joined Carers UK, and then I found Carers Bromley. They ran a group every Thursday, but it was only for the carer; I couldn't take my husband with me.'

What Lalita really wanted was to find a place where she and her husband could mix with other people from the Asian community, a place where they could come together to socialise and to support each other. But in Bromley in south London where they lived, Lalita found no appropriate dedicated community services catering for Asian elders. 'I told Carers Bromley, "There's nothing for Asian carers in this area." Their worker came round to my house, and she said, "I can't set a group up, but I can help you do it." So, I thought, "Let me open up a place." It took me three years, running about. I went shop to shop, everywhere, asking for support. Carers Bromley helped me to get the first grant of £5,000.'

Lalita didn't set out to establish her own organisation, but she recognised a need and felt sure that she could do something that would be of benefit to herself and her husband, as well as many others like them. A little encouragement was all she needed to decide that this was an idea she had to turn into a reality. And so in 1999, the Bromley Asian Cultural Association began to meet on a Tuesday in the back room of the United Reformed Church. At the beginning, there were ten members, but BACA now has 120 members with at least fifty attending each week for lunch. The majority of the members are older people and their carers, many of whom are elderly themselves. But, as Lalita explained, BACA welcomes all ages and all cultures:

Gujarati, Punjabi, South Indian and Sri Lankan, Hindu, Sikh, Muslim and Christian. 'As far as I am concerned, we are all one. Everyone is together, there are no conflicts; we all have the same interests. When I put the price of food up from 50p to £1, everyone jumps up to complain together!'

As the club began to grow, Lalita set about developing the skills she needed to run the organisation, such as keeping accounts, writing funding applications and producing reports. She has been able to secure funding to expand its services, employ staff and build links with community groups and local services. But throughout this growth, she has been hands-on in all aspects of the club, working to build a warm, friendly, supportive place, accessible to all who need it. In fact, for the first six years, Lalita herself shopped for and cooked all the hot meals provided by the club, until council funding enabled her to employ cooks.

BACA has always been primarily a place to get together socially with others from the Asian community. But over the years, Lalita has built up a range of activities, depending on what funding has been available, giving members the opportunities to enjoy IT classes, English classes, swimming lessons, sewing, aromatherapy, yoga and exercise sessions. The club also provides a vital mechanism to allow elders in the community to access relevant services and support. Five years ago, as a result of research into low take-up of health services by Asian elders in the borough, the local primary care trust began to work much more closely with BACA. Health visitors now provide regular talks on health issues (which Lalita translates into Hindi and Gujarati), and once a month two nurses visit and provide health checks.

BACA now works closely with other ethnic-minority community organisations in Bromley and has particularly close links with the Pineapple Lunch Club: a group set up and run by Caribbean elders. As a result of a local community development project, the groups come together to support each other, work together to campaign for more stable funding and share their knowledge about ways to negotiate effectively with the local council. Members visit each other's clubs, and this year they will be key participants in the borough's first 'Celebration of Diversity' day. Lalita wanted me to understand how important it is to enable people to have opportunities to spend time with others from their own communities, people who speak their language and understand their customs. This gives people a sense of security and belonging, she explained, which is a foundation that then allows them to reach out and do things together with people from other communities and cultures.

I asked Lalita why she does all that she does, and she told me simply, 'I like to help people. We always used to help people. My husband used to help everyone: he was happy going everywhere, running around, and then he was happy for me to do it.' Lalita's efforts have built a club that reaches out to many in her local Asian community and beyond. But throughout the development and expansion of BACA, Lalita was always focused primarily on providing the best for her husband, the motivation that led to BACA's creation in the first place. She explained that this was a place where he was happy, a place he liked to be, and told me how he enjoyed helping in the running of the club, despite his disabilities. She laughed, 'He used to fight with people if they moved the chairs out of the line he'd put them in. People wanted to move the chairs into smaller groups, and he would get angry with them.'

Lalita knows that the club continues to make a difference to many people's lives, just as it did for her husband during his last years. Many members travel quite some distance to come to BACA, evidence for her of the need it is fulfilling. 'One member comes from Orpington. She's eighty-five and is on crutches. The club pays for her travel costs to get here. She tells me how much she looks forward to coming here every Tuesday. Another two ladies also like that – over eighty, lonely and disabled – they want to come and communicate with people who understand them. I pay their transport costs. They are so lonely. They don't know English, but when they get here they can mix up with other people like them. It's working OK for them.'

For many elderly members of the local community who may be lonely or isolated, suffering from illness or disability, or who struggle to find accessible, inclusive opportunities to come together with others who share their interests, needs and experiences, BACA is a lifeline. But beyond being a place where people can meet or find support, it is a place of fun and celebration. Lalita talked about the celebrations the club members hold for Christmas, Divali and Vaisakhi. Every member cooks food and brings something to share, and the local mayor and chief of police are invited, together with local voluntary sector groups. The evening is an opportunity to celebrate and to learn about each other's cultures and faiths. 'The fact that we always invited the mayor to our cultural events has meant that there is a better understanding at the council of the needs of the Asian community.' In recognition of her tireless efforts for her community, in 2006 Lalita was very proud to win an award from the mayor for voluntary service to the borough.

Lalita's husband died earlier this year. During the last months of his life, she devoted herself to caring for him, but now, despite a knee operation, she continues to be involved in the Alzheimer's Society, Advocacy Alliance, Carers Bromley and the local Age Concern Hour Bank, where she does knitting for people with disabilities and contributes to a poetry class. Her daughters are keen that she should slow down, and she has now resigned as chair of BACA, but her enthusiasm and energy continue to touch all those around her. 'I don't know how to pass my time. I've been so busy all my life. And another thing, I'm very independent. I don't like to rely on anyone; I like to do what I can do myself. Sometimes I can't go to BACA because I have a hospital appointment. When I don't go, the next week there's a riot: "Where did you go last week, you were not here, we missed you!"'

13

JACQUI NASUH

From feeling worthless and hopeless and helpless, now some of the women are going to university like my daughter. They're doing brilliant things with their lives.

Jacqui Nasuh is the founder of Chrysalis Domestic Violence Services in Liverpool. She is right at the frontline in helping those experiencing domestic violence and their children.

Jacqui has her own experience of the anguish that domestic violence can cause and saw at first hand why Chrysalis was needed. 'I, myself, had grown up with domestic violence. My father was extremely violent and in those days you couldn't call the police. It was horrendous. My school life was deeply affected. I never went to school. I used to hide in the coal cupboard. You think, as a child, as long as you're around, you can save your mum. It affects you in many ways.'

But Jacqui's is ultimately a story rooted in a mother's anger. What drove her to take action was her horror when, seven years ago, her own daughter began to experience domestic violence. 'My daughter got involved with a violent control freak, a young man who was very controlling and very violent. She was only seventeen. She had been thrown over a hedge, she'd had her hair pulled out and been punched and kicked. When we phoned the police and explained she knew the guy, as they had been out on a date, the police said, "Well, it's domestic. You need to phone the domestic violence unit." I phoned the domestic violence unit and they said that there was nothing they could do. It was up to my daughter to complain. I explained that she was only seventeen and that this chap was really violent and dangerous and she was too scared to make any complaint. But they said that there was nothing they could do unless my daughter complained. I was quite shocked. A few years earlier, when my daughter was only fifteen, somebody tried to drag her into a car. When we told the police, they pulled out all the stops to get this guy. It was on the local news and the radio and everything. I thought, "Well, just because this guy's known to her, does that make a difference? Shouldn't it be treated like it's serious?" It was just as serious as this other incident and yet was treated completely differently.'

For most of us, our families are our most important source of love and care, and home is the place where we are nurtured and supported and protected. So when the family home is no longer a safe place, no longer a place of care but of fear, the impact can be devastating. It takes love and care and consistent, ongoing, one-to-one support to help to rebuild a life shattered when our most fundamental trusts have been betrayed. It takes the kind of remarkable commitment shown by volunteers across the country, a commitment exemplified in the work of Jacqui and the Chrysalis team.

Domestic violence is a crime that is often hidden away and under-reported, yet it still accounts for around 16 per cent of all reported violent crime in the UK. It is rarely a one-off incident and can continue over time before the perpetrator is stopped. And, as Jacqui discovered when trying to find help for her daughter and supporting her to pursue her complex case through the legal system, many of those who experience domestic violence struggle to ask for and access appropriate support.

'I just wasn't willing to accept it. I thought, "There are lots of other women and girls who are suffering in this way." When I approached the police to voice my concerns, they said to me, "There are only two police officers covering the whole of the north-west of Merseyside in domestic violence." So I said it wasn't good enough, and I developed our project from there. I just went out into the community. I began to talk about the issues. I was invited to speak at a big community awards event and lots of people came forward saying I or my daughter or my sister went through this. I got volunteers together, local women who were all concerned about the same issues. Some had experiences of court cases being dropped, not knowing when their partners were on bail, where they were. I was uncovering loads of horror stories similar to my daughter's. I got the women together and thought, "What do we do about this?"'

Jacqui began to build up a network of volunteers and apply for small grants, and she set up the Chrysalis project in a local community centre. From these initial efforts, Jacqui has grown Chrysalis Domestic Violence Services into an established organisation, run entirely by volunteers, providing one-to-one drop-in support for women who are experiencing domestic violence. 'Women come to us, mostly by word of mouth, for a variety of support. It could be that they're looking for a solicitor, help with housing, legal issues, contact arrangements with the children, anything really. Domestic violence can produce a lot of problems in the family, so they come to us for all kinds of support.'

More recently, Chrysalis has been running the 'Freedom Programme', which enables victims of violence to understand what is happening to them and focuses particularly on understanding the effects of violence on their children. 'We run the group twice a week, funded by Sure Start, which enables us to reach young families now. We think the Freedom Programme is a very good tool to help women not only recognise the violence and tactics used by the perpetrator but also help them to move on. They find it very hard to be able to break away from the violence, so even if they stay in these violent relationships, we try and help the men to seek help as well.'

While Jacqui's work began as a response to what she saw as gaps in statutory provision, over the years she has increasingly sought to work in partnership with local statutory agencies, trying to make sure the experiences and expertise that Chrysalis has built up is used to help everyone working to deliver improved services for local families. 'At the start, we didn't have a good name with the police. We were seen as a thorn in their side, because we were quite outspoken. We decided to have a launch event to celebrate our achievements and let the police know what was happening. Senior police officers attended the launch, and from there we established much better relations. We've raised our profile with the police, and we've received funding from them to open up a forum. We've worked hard for, and earned, our credibility with the police. Working alongside the police and social services and other big organisations that come to us for advice is a big achievement. We started off challenging negative attitudes, and now we've turned it around and work very closely with them in order to build up support networks for women and their families. So, where a family is in need, especially the children, we help wherever we can. We never, ever turn anybody away.'

Looking back over seven years of work, Jacqui reflected on the impact that the Chrysalis project has had. 'There are big changes in Liverpool. I won't say that it's us that's done it, but it's people like ourselves who've been proactive and got out there and raised awareness with the police and the courts. The impact of our work has been that we've raised awareness of this issue.'

But most important to Jacqui and to the volunteers she works with are the individual lives that have been touched: the one-to-one support that helps families rebuild shattered lives. 'We've lost count of the hundreds of women we have helped. We're proud of the women who've been able to turn their lives around, like my daughter has. My daughter has a little baby girl and she's at college, hoping to go to university.

She runs the groups with me now. She works in the local youth club, running programmes for young people on prevention, because prevention is better than cure, isn't it? She's working with local women and shares her own experiences and her own story. She's an inspiration to the women: she's a lovely girl, and people don't believe what she's been through. She has an impact on young women. She inspires them to break away and do something better with their lives. I'm proud that she's taken on our work, which, at the end of the day, started with her and now she's taking it forward. From feeling worthless and hopeless and helpless, now some of the women are going to university like my daughter. They're doing brilliant things with their lives.'

14

MANDY JETTER

We can see all these people as individuals. To us, they're not just numbers, they're not a big headache, if you like; they're individuals who are well worth respecting and, just like any of us, have a right to be treated with compassion and respect.

M andy Jetter's father was a refugee who arrived alone in Britain in the 1930s as a teenage boy, sent by his family to escape the horrors of Nazi-occupied Europe. He spent most of his working life at a school in the East End of London, where his contribution to the community was so great that when he died the school named a newly built wing in his honour. 'I like the idea that, as a refugee, he'd been given a chance and in return he made a huge contribution to a part of London, to the point that he was so highly thought of that they bothered to name a building after him,' explained Mandy.

So when, in the 1990s, Mandy became aware of the plight of Bosnians fleeing civil war, she decided from her Newcastle home that she would help refugees in need of support and security, and she decided on a unique course of action: to use her interest in gardening to make a difference.

By the mid-1990s, Newcastle was host to many Bosnian refugees who had fled the conflict in the Balkans. Having heard on the radio about a therapeutic gardening project being run by the Medical Foundation for the Care of Victims of Torture, and being a keen gardener herself, Mandy wondered whether she could secure an allotment so that some of the refugees could enjoy growing their own fruit, vegetables and flowers. Following an attack on their community centre, some of the key members of the little Bosnian community moved to London and the project stalled. But in 2000, when the Government adopted a new policy of dispersing asylum seekers to different parts of the UK, Mandy picked up the idea again. 'I was able to get a little bit of funding from the Health Action Zone and from a couple of trusts, so it was very much a shoestring budget, but that's how I started off.'

With the help of some friends and the Newcastle Council for Voluntary Service, she set about raising funds and building a core of support for what she called the Comfrey Project. 'I was warmed by the number of people, very busy people, who were prepared to listen to me. As long as it was slightly more than a half-baked idea, they were prepared to listen and give me feedback, and that was how I derived the initial support to set it up. I thought it would be terribly difficult, a daunting thing, to set up a constitution and establish a charity. I got a group of people together: initially they were a management committee and then, when we became a charity, they became trustees. We named our charity Comfrey because it is the name of a plant traditionally used in healing, a plant that nourishes other plants. I was thinking about healing in all its senses.'

The Comfrey Project now has allotments at three sites: two in Newcastle and one in Gateshead. Its forty-five members are drawn from many different countries. Throughout the year, they meet weekly at two of the sites, while the third site is for members who want to come and go as they please or who have moved on in their confidence and no longer need the regular organised support of the project. As well as tending the allotments, members enjoy other activities such as cooking and visiting places of interest in the local area, all designed to help disoriented and at times fearful people feel more confident and secure in their new environment.

Through gardening, Mandy is working to give people who feel dislocated and uprooted a way to feel at home again, and to give those suffering from isolation and anxiety a way to find some peace in their lives. 'The aim, really, is to provide a place where people can feel safe, where they can feel respected, listened to, supported and believed. I think it's all those elements we take pretty much for granted ourselves and which are lacking in the lives of asylum seekers and refugees. Ultimately, what we're trying to help them achieve is a sense of normality. Eating and growing what you eat are universal activities, and for these people who are leading very abnormal existences it can restore – even for a few hours a week – a sense of normality. At the moment, people whose asylum claims fail are being removed very speedily, and what's difficult is sometimes when you come back to the allotment you see where people have sown stuff but they have been taken away and we don't know whether we're going to see them again. They lead such fragmented lives, with so much uncertainty. For me, as someone who loves gardening, there has always been a very sharp contrast between that wonderful predictability of the cycle of the seasons – of germination, growth, harvest, dying down and then all the planning and starting again – and the lives of the individuals who come to the allotments.'

Newcastle has a citywide support group for asylum seekers and refugees, an informal multi-agency network which helps the Comfrey Project and others share information and lobby effectively. Comfrey's members come by referral from GPs, from mental-health workers, teachers and each other. Members are encouraged to bring other members of their family or friends, and often they then become project users in their own right. As Mandy and her colleagues, one of whom is originally from Bosnia, have always wanted, it is slowly becoming an established part of life in Newcastle. 'Given that asylum seekers have traditionally had quite a bad name, we've never had any hostility from other allotment holders. I'd say initially we were viewed with a little bit of suspicion, a bit of scepticism, I suppose, but now we feel very much part of the furniture, and I think people have got used to us. One real example of how we feel we fit in now is that the allotment association in the west end of the city actually nominated us for a competition across all the allotments in Newcastle, and we won first prize. In fact, two years running we got first prize for best group allotment, and that was wonderful for us. We won £50 and were able to go out and spend it on plants. Of course, it wasn't about the money or even the pride in winning the prize because the allotment was looking so good. It was about being accepted, and that was somewhat more profound than simply getting a prize. It was a quiet, subtle way of saying, "Yes, actually we are integrated."'

The experience of leaving your home and seeking asylum can rob a person of so much of their identity and sense of self. For Mandy, this is at the heart of what motivates her to keep going with the project. 'I think we're lucky because we can see all these people as individuals. To us, they're not just numbers, they're not a big headache, if you like; they're individuals who are well worth respecting and, just like any of us, have a right to be treated with compassion and respect.'

Mandy's care and respect for each individual who comes to the project is clear when she begins to talk about her members. She tells the story of one woman, an Ethiopian of Eritrean origin whose father had been killed as a result of his political activity and whose husband had also been arrested. Although not involved in politics herself, she knew she was at risk and went into hiding with her small son, eventually escaping to Sudan and then to England. 'Just to give you an idea of the sort of existence she'd led before coming to England, she told me that when she was in a hostel in London, before being sent to Newcastle, there was a knock on her door and her little boy instinctively went and hid under the bed: he was that fearful in spite of the fact that he was now in England. It turned out to be the woman from the room next door asking to borrow something. She's been in Newcastle for six years now and she's still waiting for the conclusion of her case. To me, she exemplifies a lot of the characteristics of our project users, and that is a huge level of stoicism, patience and real courage. They have very uncertain futures and many of them are incredibly homesick, but they still, somehow, keep going. I don't know if it's something to do with being part of a group or working in lovely surroundings on the allotments, especially in summer, but there's a lot of very good humour and the atmosphere is quite dynamic, there are a lot of dynamic conversations. So, although there are lows, there are also a lot of highs. In spite of all that's happened to them, they retain the core essence of who they are, and to me that's quite remarkable. I've got enormous respect for them.'

Mandy tells another story of a man who, after six years, was told his application for asylum had been accepted. 'He told me that after he opened the letter he'd had to read it nine times because he couldn't believe what was written there and, of course, because it's written in quite complicated legal terms. It was lovely when he came to the allotment to tell us; it was wonderful.'

But even that is often not the end of the story. 'When people do get indefinite leave to remain and can start to rebuild their lives, when they realise they now have a future in this country, suddenly the past can flood back. So while they consider themselves to be incredibly fortunate and are the envy of those who are still going through the asylum process, they also feel they have come down to earth with a thud. It sounds odd, but it's at that point that people can go downhill, because they remember what they've lost. They allow themselves to remember what they've left behind, and that's not just material things and family; it's their standing in their own community, their social networks, their identity – and all that floods back.'

In her modest and softly spoken way, Mandy has fought courageously to tackle prejudice and to offer comfort, stability and a sense of belonging to some of the most vulnerable people in our communities. Like many small charities, funding has been a source of persistent uncertainty, but now, as the Comfrey Project continues to provide vital support, she is confident of its future. 'The toughest thing has been getting funds. You do get knocked back a lot and funding has been a difficult one for us: getting known and constantly reminding people that we're around is a struggle. We've had years of just keeping our heads above water, but now we're into a new funding phase, thankfully. After going for six years, we've got two years of funding security, which is excellent. I feel we're on the map now, but it's been a question of just keeping at it and keeping going.'

Looking back on her experiences, Mandy knows she has been offered an insight into the realities facing refugees and asylum seekers that most of us will never have. And this insight leaves her with an important message. 'Although it's faded a bit, the vilification of asylum seekers in the press makes me wish that more people would stand up and say, "Look, this isn't on. You can't talk about people in this way." I've never experienced hearing somebody important having the courage to stand up for such vulnerable people. It's easy for me, because I'm lucky: I meet them several times a week and I can see them for who they are as individuals. But that's certainly a message I'd want to put across: put yourself in these people's shoes, try to make an effort to understand the trauma that they are going through, try and listen – I think that's really important.'

15

PATRICK FRIEL

There are hundreds of people like me who are supported through the system now, probably thousands. Getting involved as a volunteer was my way of giving something back.

At the age of only sixteen, Patrick Friel was studying for an NVQ in business administration while working nearly full time and living independently in his own flat rented from a social landlord. A problem with his housing benefit claim meant that Patrick's rent fell into arrears, and, after a time, he was threatened with eviction. A mentor at his training course suggested that Patrick contact the Streetwise Community Law Centre in Penge, south-east London. 'Basically they were going to evict me; my housing benefit was all messed up. I came to Streetwise and they sorted out all the housing benefit forms, got everything backdated to where it should have been, and that solved that problem . . . or so I thought.'

Patrick continued to live independently and progressed in his studies until, at eighteen, he experienced further problems with his housing. 'Then they closed my case again. The people that housed me seemed to forget that they had housed me in their property; they didn't put me on the housing list as they were supposed to, therefore I didn't get moved. So, when I came to the age of eighteen and a half, they just said, "Oh look, you're too old now", and they just closed the case.' After further follow-up by the advisers at Streetwise, the issue was resolved, allowing Patrick to move into a permanent home in independent rented accommodation.

Around this time, after Streetwise had resolved his second set of complex difficulties with accommodation, Patrick became a volunteer at the organisation and a member of its management committee. Now, at twenty-one, he is giving his time to make sure other people get the kind of support that helped him to turn his life around.

Patrick is a perfect example of a great truth: that we all need help at some time in our lives. He has been helped by, and now helps, one of the many dedicated organisations across the country that are working to ensure we get the assistance we need. It can be easy, once we get through tough times, to want to move on and put the past behind us. But some of the most inspiring people I have met are those who, having received help during particularly difficult times in their own lives, don't just turn away but work to give something back to the organisations or causes that were there for them, those people who want to make sure that others can receive the help they valued so much.

When Patrick was invited to join the management committee of the Community Law Centre by his own caseworker, Roselle, he readily agreed. As he explained, it was because of their one-to-one relationship, because he was asked by someone he knew and trusted, that he was willing to get involved. 'I wanted to join the management committee. I thought it was a good service, and I don't think that enough people are aware of it: word needs to be spread. It's good for other young people to get their views across and Streetwise is very young-people-orientated.'

As many organisations find, it is often those people who have used and benefited from their services that can become their most important volunteers. Their first-hand understanding of the issues involved brings invaluable expertise, and their own stories and experiences can help to motivate staff and users alike. Now Patrick is making sure others can get the help that benefited him so greatly. 'There was a colleague at work that I referred to Streetwise. She was having housing problems, she had just had a baby and was on maternity leave, there were complications with finances, and everything got really confusing and messed up and she sort of lost it because she was going to get evicted. Vivienne managed to sort out her housing issues. Vivienne is one of the mobile workers that I helped to recruit, so I referred a friend to get advice from a worker I had recruited and interviewed. She's fine now: all her housing issues have been resolved. I told her to come to Streetwise, she came in, and they sorted everything out.'

Using this and other stories, he explained what made him so committed to the work of Streetwise and other community law centres: a belief that effective early intervention, and simply getting the right professional advice to young people at the right time in their lives, can achieve good results at a comparatively low cost rather than letting issues accumulate until crisis point is reached.

Because Patrick was one of the first young people to get involved in the running of the law centre, his engagement has spurred them on to do much more work directly involving the young service users and changing the work of the agency overall. And for Patrick personally there have been many developments. 'I think there are a lot of things I wouldn't have done without Streetwise, to be honest. I wouldn't have recruited anyone, I had never been on a panel before; it's good to be on a committee, just to get the feel of that; and also speaking at a conference and doing sponsored walks – basically just being involved, really.'

And, as Patrick explained, his motivation is very simple. 'Well, I know how much I was helped. I know where I am now and where I would have been otherwise, so that keeps me going. I know what they do, and I know what it's for. There are hundreds of people like me who are supported through the system now, probably thousands. Getting involved as a volunteer was my way of giving something back.'

The personal, one-to-one support Patrick has received from the staff at Streetwise has been key to his own development and to his ongoing commitment to the work. 'I'm inspired by the staff, Elaine, Roselle and the others. They are really keen, they really go out of their way, put in more hours than anyone would expect, despite other family commitments, and you know they'd take a bullet for those young people. They go to the nth degree while also trying to run a service.'

Patrick was so positive about his experiences as a volunteer and a great advocate of just how much we each have to gain from giving a little back. 'I think people should get involved, as it makes them more aware of what's going on. I am a lot more aware of everything now, on both sides, being a client and on the management committee as well, so I have a bird's-eye view of everything. It has given me a lot more knowledge, and it has definitely helped my work. I am a lot more confident at work, and I have progressed in my studies. I just know exactly where I stand.

'When I thought I was going to be evicted from my flat, I thought I might have to give up my studies, go full time and get stuck in a dead-end job somewhere. But now I've finished my qualification and have a good job in an international courier company. I have been promoted. I'm going travelling for four months, but my employers have agreed to keep my job open for me, and I'm going to come back and find a house. So it's a little different. It's a really good advert for the stuff that you get out of it yourself as well as the stuff about helping other people.'

Patrick has gone far in changing his own life and he has moved from someone who was in need of a little bit of help to someone now helping others. And with each new opportunity that opens up to him, he is finding new ways to support an organisation that was there at the moment he needed them and that daily delivers practical assistance to those who face difficulties.

16

HELEN ATKINS

I resigned from my job in the City without any idea
of what I wanted to do apart from doing something
useful . . . My [adoptive] parents wanted to help
someone else, so they took me on board . . . and
it would seem a bit selfish to then just go and make
lots of money for myself.

Helen Atkins gave up a successful career in the City to
help run the Poppy Project: an organisation providing
support and housing to women who have been trafficked into
prostitution in Britain. I was interested to find out why she had
made such a move.

'I was adopted into a white family. I'm half-Jamaican
myself,' Helen explained. 'I was brought up in a very happy
environment. My parents were a doctor and nurse. I've got
three siblings, all of whom work in caring professions, and my
sister's a twenty-four-hour carer for her husband, my brother-
in-law, who has cerebral palsy. One of my brothers lectures in
permaculture and sustainable agriculture – caring for the earth
rather than people – and the other brother is a political activist.
So we are all very socially aware. I can't imagine what my life
would have been like had I not been adopted but instead kept
in an environment where I was the unwanted product of a
one-night stand. My parents wanted to help someone else, so
they took me on board and gave me a very happy, privileged
upbringing. I got the opportunity to do music, sport, whatever,

and had an excellent education. And it would seem a bit selfish to then just go and make lots of money for myself.'

A childhood ambition to become a barrister led to a law degree at Christ's College, Cambridge, but Helen eventually opted instead for a career in the City. She was working as a research analyst for Futures International until, in September 2002, she made a choice that was to change her life. 'I resigned from my job in the City without any idea of what I wanted to do apart from doing something useful and knowing that the only way to get into the voluntary sector was to volunteer.'

In that one moment, Helen decided to take a risk and turn her life around by committing to using her skills for good, though for what purpose, she didn't quite yet know. She joined her local Amnesty International group and volunteered at the Charities Advisory Trust, which brought her into contact with many issues that concerned her, and the organisations who were working on them. But it was a night out at the Rio Cinema in Dalston, east London, that Helen points to as her personal turning point. 'A double bill was showing of *Dirty Pretty Things* and *Lilya 4-Ever*, a film by Swedish director Lukas Moodysson examining the issues of modern-day slavery: women trafficked to work in the sex industry. *Lilya 4-Ever* was very harrowing. I came out feeling depressed but also strangely uplifted, because I thought I'd finally found exactly what I wanted to do, what I wanted to stop, in effect. It really was just like that.'

Helen had no direct experience of trafficking and prostitution, no immediate reason to commit herself to this cause. But, as she explained, it has been her family and her childhood that have inspired the decisions that have shaped her life. 'Being half-Jamaican, I've always had an interest in slavery and issues involving race and ethnicity. I found out that I was put up for adoption at fifteen months old because of the colour of my skin. So race issues, my minority ethnic background, slavery: that was all of interest to me.'

And so, determined to do something about the issue, Helen

researched organisations working in the field and found the Poppy Project, which had been developed as an initiative within Eaves Housing Association. Eaves have been providing supported housing for vulnerable women in London for thirty years and through their work became aware of women who had been brought into the UK to be forced into prostitution. In 2003, the Poppy Project was set up with funding from the Home Office. In four years, it has helped nearly 650 women from sixty different countries in five continents.

Helen was clear that she had found an organisation she wanted to be part of, but it took determination and perseverance before she was given an opportunity to get involved. 'I emailed and said I'd like to come and volunteer for them, but they said, "Sorry, not at the moment." I was very disappointed, but there wasn't another organisation working on these issues.

'A year later, I'd been trying to educate myself about the subject and was feeling quite determined. I emailed them again and said, "I'm aware that this issue is growing. I'm looking at your newsletters and you've got more work than you can deal with. I'm really keen to help if I can." They were just taking on volunteers for the first time, but it wasn't simply that I really wanted to come and they let me in. It was a three-month process and the most rigorous interview I'd ever been through, which made me think, "What am I getting into?" But it has to be that way because of the nature of the work. It's not just a question of someone turning up on the door; it's a very sensitive situation. You have to have an enhanced Criminal Records Bureau check, which can take up to six months. So I applied in October 2005 and started in January 2006.'

From being a volunteer, Helen now works full time at the Poppy Project and is responsible for researching good practice and developing the project's services. The work of the Poppy Project is difficult to encapsulate, as there is no typical case: each woman's needs determine the support made available. Helen explained that project workers will work towards identifying longer-term medical needs, psychological needs and physical needs as soon as they can, but in the first instance, practical support is what is required. 'The office is very secure. We've got lots and lots of locks and security. We're right next to a police station, so the women should automatically feel safer than they did. And then we sit them down and give them a cup of hot sweet tea and something to eat – whatever they want. We have supplies of clothes in the office. We can provide something comfortable to wear like a cosy tracksuit, little things that are going to make them feel a bit better. And then we have toiletries and make-up – everything they will need; often it really helps to wash your face and brush your hair.

'The police will be involved, getting a statement and trying to work out if there are other people in immediate danger. We're keen to not put the women under too much pressure in the opening stages. We just spend time with them and assess if they are suicidal. It's really about working out the best order in which to do things and what is the most pressing need – gauging their state of being, trying to listen as much as possible. Usually referrals can't speak English, certainly not well enough to communicate on the level that we need to, so we call in a specialist female translator, which can be expensive and take time. Sexual health obviously is a big issue, which requires a lot of sensitive care. We look into things such as counselling. Often it's a very long process for them to be able to talk about what's happened and be ready for counselling. So, in between, we act as a shoulder to cry on.

'Then one of the most important things is supported housing: safe housing at a secure location. It's essential that they feel safe and not threatened by anyone round them. Once the basic things have been sorted out – accommodation and health – we begin to look at perhaps training, education. And there's a voluntary return scheme through which we provide the women with assistance to relocate back to their country of origin. We help them with legal advice and advocacy, supporting them if they are willing to cooperate with the police to testify against the trafficker, then supporting them through that process. We help them with claims for asylum if they don't want to go home. It's pretty much an endless list.'

Helen and the Poppy Project team offer vital support to women who have had their dignity, identity and freedom stripped away and been left without a home, vulnerable, alone and with nothing. Left broken and traumatised, these women need intensive support simply to be safe, let alone to begin to rebuild their lives. From Helen's descriptions, it became clear that the work of the Poppy team is relentless, often distressing, and requires round-the-clock care and dedication. 'If they need to go to hospital, then we go with them to hospital. If their immediate medical health's OK, then we can eventually take them to one of the safe houses where they have a clean room, and they're really very nice places to stay. They have their own bedsit. They don't have to share, but there are other people around in the building who have been through similar experiences. So a lot of bonding goes on in the houses as well. And then we ensure that there is constant monitoring, constant contact, constant checks and visits. Each service user has their own support worker, and they can contact them twenty-four hours a day. We also have someone who's on, as it were, out of hours. Each evening throughout the night until the morning someone will be on call, so if there's an emergency at one of the houses, someone is immediately contactable to sort it out. It requires a lot of patience and some sleepless nights, but it's the only way to do it.'

Whilst acknowledging the considerable difficulties involved in the work, Helen speaks with animation and passion about the work of the project and the urgent need to tackle the issues that underlie their work. From challenging beginnings, she described how she has grown in her role. 'This is a very holistic place to work. What the organisation can get from you is equal to what you can get from the organisation, and personal development is very important. When I started, I was very much in at the deep end. I think the subject itself has been a steep learning curve, and it continues. The more you learn about what is going on, the more you understand it's actually a bit of an insoluble problem. Now, that's all the more reason to work towards diminishing it, but it's an issue with a global reach and yet such a local problem. The migration aspects, poverty, all these things that people have been trying to tackle for centuries, are combined in the work we do in the Poppy Project.'

This understanding of the wider context in which she operates and the complex social factors that are contributing to the problems she is seeking to tackle is vital to Helen's work. While the Poppy Project is focused primarily on dealing with the consequences of this shameful trade, Helen is determined to campaign to tackle the causes.

'The most important thing in terms of tackling the problem is demand and society's responsibility in fostering that. Demand for prostitution is rising. We are looking at a cultural shift. The rise of the Internet means that men don't have to skulk around street corners and be branded as kerb crawlers; they can order a woman on the Internet from their living room pretty much like a pizza. This means that the risk factor for them has been removed. Then you've got low-cost air travel, meaning that stag parties go away to cheap Eastern European countries and have the confidence to buy sex for the first time, and then they come back and have the confidence to continue. And then the media is a whole subject in itself: the whole "lads' mags" attitudes mean that sexual exploitation is becoming more acceptable. About 80 per cent of fifteen to seventeen year olds are exposed to hardcore pornography, often accidentally on the Internet, but that has an effect on attitudes towards what's acceptable and what's not. The age-old debate about whether prostitution is occupation or oppression is never going to be reconciled. But again and again, statistics researched from all over the world, including the UK, show that the majority of women in prostitution are exploited and abused on a regular basis. Seventy per cent of survivors of prostitution suffer from post-traumatic stress disorder in the same category as war veterans or victims of state-organised torture.'

Helen shows remarkable enthusiasm for work that is clearly highly challenging, often disturbing and largely thankless. She is aware of the scale of the problem she is trying to tackle and the immense challenges involved in any attempts to deal with the underlying causes that must be addressed if there is to be any hope of a comprehensive, lasting solution. I wondered what it was that keeps her going when faced with some of the worst aspects of humanity and when hope is often in short supply. 'It probably sounds a bit trite, but there's not really much back-slapping that goes on; good news is quite rare – without wanting to sound too negative. But Fleur, one of the service users, recently gave birth. I'd never seen her smile. Since she had the baby, she's beaming from ear to ear every time we see her, and that's really uplifting. A couple of other service users sometimes come in to have a chat, and there's kids running around. It's always uplifting. In a trafficking situation, it can be the case that women have enforced terminations, non-medical ones as well, some really, really awful occurrences. Or they may have the baby and then it's taken away. The baby might be trafficked itself. So to see the settled life continuing, I guess, is something to clutch onto.'

As the UK marks the 200th anniversary of the Parliamentary Act that led to the abolition of the slave trade, the trafficking of women is evidence that a form of slavery continues in this country. Despite the enormous progress we have made over the centuries in protecting the fundamental rights of all those who live and work here, this shocking reality must remain at the very forefront of our conscience and our concern. As Helen reminded me, above all we must never be satisfied or complacent as a country until we can be assured that the most vulnerable in our society have the protection and support they need and that the freedom we pride ourselves on is genuinely upheld as the right of all.

17

PAUL HURLEY

The process of immigration is not easy, but I am able
to come in at the end of that and hopefully help make
things better. This is a really positive thing, and it's
about real people rather than statistics.

B ased in Cardiff, Paul Hurley certainly lives a busy life:
'I'm an artist, I make performance art and run a small
arts organisation, and I'm doing a PhD, and I work as a waiter
. . . that's basically it.' But in the midst of all this, Paul makes
time to volunteer as a mentor with Time Together, a national
refugee mentoring project that matches UK citizens with
refugees in one-to-one mentoring relationships. As Paul's story
illustrates, individuals with a social conscience are using their
own skills to mentor and support people finding it difficult to
adjust to life in our country.

Paul's involvement in the project began in the arts
community and his involvement in the Big Arts Week. Run by
national volunteering charity TimeBank, this initiative invited
professional artists to volunteer their time and share their skills
to inspire local children in schools throughout the country.
When TimeBank later got in touch looking for volunteers
for their refugee mentoring scheme Time Together, Paul was
excited to get involved: 'It just sounded like a great project,
and this work can only happen on a human level.'

Following training in mentoring and refugee issues, Time
Together selects individuals to be paired based on relevant

interests or skills and what the mentee's objectives are. Paul was introduced to Othman, a musician from Sudan. Othman arrived in the UK five years ago after being forced out of Sudan. Now working in security, Othman was formerly a highly successful musician, one of the top ten musicians in Sudan, Paul told me. Their shared interest in the arts has been an important element of their mentoring relationship, and Paul has worked to help Othman navigate the complexities of his new situation.

Paul explained, 'The Time Together project can really help individuals who are adjusting to permanent life in this country and dealing with not only the transition from where they've been living before but also quite often trauma or whatever's happened before they've come to this country. I think working with or having a relationship with a British citizen can be incredibly helpful, both on an emotional level and on a very practical level of knowing how to do little things that we might not think twice about. So, sometimes we just meet to chat, but other times I'll help him do very practical things he wants to do, like going to the bank.'

We talked about what it took to be a good mentor, and Paul told me it meant 'listening, patience, recognising someone's needs, and then being able to help them achieve their goals'. And as their relationship has developed, Paul has been able to do just this. 'I have been able to help Othman realise some of his ambitions and enable him to perhaps see that they can be realised. He's a very good musician; he's been running a group doing traditional Sudanese dance and performance with children. They've been doing it for a couple of years informally, and over the past few months I've helped him constitute the group formally and make an application for Arts Council funding to do a big performance in the autumn. That's been great for me, using my experience and contacts in the arts here in Cardiff that he doesn't have access to.'

Mentoring allows Paul to draw on his strengths and experiences, and also offers a flexibility that suits him well.

'Although there is the structured support offered by Time Together and SOVA [a local volunteering organisation], most of what Othman and I have been doing has been completely independent of that. It's really amazing just how much can be achieved with this liberation of structure. We can go a couple of weeks without meeting, and then we can meet for a whole day or an evening and do things organically in a way that fits our relationship and our circumstances. I think that's one of the reasons why the project works best on a voluntary basis; if it was carried out by social services, it would be restrained by bureaucracy.'

But even given this flexibility, mentoring is an intensive and long-term commitment, and I was interested to understand what motivated someone like Paul, who has so much else going on in his life, to get involved. 'I thought it was a very interesting and worthy project to get involved in. I'd been thinking about doing some volunteering work, and this just seemed exactly the sort of thing that I wanted to do: something that's not really connected to any particular aim in terms of a job, or business or career. You're helping somebody else and helping a community by doing it, that's the main objective; you're not doing it for anybody else's benefit other than the parties involved.

'I'm finding a balance between what I do for my own needs or desires or career or advancement and then actually doing something that's for somebody else. That's a really liberating experience, and I find particularly working with a refugee that it's been a really humbling experience as well. It's something that I really believe in. I think refugees are in an incredibly difficult situation, which I can't even start to imagine, particularly for Othman but also for other refugees that I've met since starting the project. I feel like I'm doing something quite important in terms of helping him integrate and just befriending him. He's already dealt with far too much bureaucracy than anyone should ever have to.'

There is something unique about the one-to-one mentoring relationship, and I have seen it touch many different lives in many different settings. Part of what motivates Paul is the knowledge of how much he benefited from his own mentors. 'My inspirations and heroes are individuals that I've known or that I've met. No massive world leaders or spiritual icons but people who have mentored me. One was my tutor and another was somebody that I worked with in an arts project. When somebody is your teacher but becomes your friend, you feel answerable to them, even if they're not asking questions. It's like they've become some part of your conscience, and those sort of people are very important to me: people who are very driven and energetic, and accept their imperfections and flaws but do remarkable things nonetheless.'

The Time Together project helps to deliver practical support to refugees who are working to build a new life here. But by choosing to do this through building relationships between ordinary local residents and refugees in their area, the project is also aiming to shift public attitudes, and, for Paul, this is a critical aspect of the work. 'Improving people's attitudes towards asylum seekers and refugees is incredibly important. There's so much prejudice towards them socially it's like a double whammy. Whatever's happened to them has happened, and they've had to leave their own country and come here, where they face even more hardship once they arrive. So I think just to open up people's attitudes is all part of a wider picture that's adjusting British people to the shift that's happening in our society. This is how things are now in the world.'

What resonates particularly with Paul, and what makes this project so powerful, is that it tries to give new residents a personal and real understanding of what it is like to live in Britain. The mentors are real people with their own individual attitudes and opinions. They are not giving the 'official view' but their own honest take on life in the UK, and it is this that makes their help so valuable to those building lives here for themselves. 'There's something about the project that feels slightly subversive, which I quite enjoy. We've obviously had some very good and very funny conversations. Othman has gone through a citizenship process, but then I can actually say, "No, of course, everyone hates the tax office or everyone hates this or that." Or, "This is ridiculous, but that's just the way this country is, and it's not entirely rosy and happy every day, a lot of things are a struggle, and it's OK to say that and to hold political opinions against the Government."'

Through mentoring, Paul has found a type of volunteering that really brings out the best that he has to give. In giving not just his time but also sharing his experiences, his energy and his enthusiasm to help someone build a life in Britain, Paul is himself an example of the very best aspects of Britain. 'It has been quite an intensive process, and Othman has gone from being someone I mentored to being a real friend. The process of immigration is not easy, but I am able to come in at the end of that and hopefully help make things better. This is a really positive thing, and it's about real people rather than statistics. It's the one-to-one thing. It's all of our responsibility to help them once they're here; it's something that I totally believe in giving up my time for.'

Along with the many terrible consequences of conflict and disaster around the world, the displacement of people from their homes and their families can have lasting and devastating consequences. I am proud of this country's history of welcoming political refugees persecuted in their own countries and of our efforts to support them in rebuilding what are often shattered lives. For those who have left everything behind, the flight from persecution is just the beginning. Building a new life from scratch and settling into British culture, with all its complexities, requires the tailored services and one-to-one support in which our voluntary organisations excel. Their vital work depends on the thousand small acts of kindness shown every day by volunteers such as Paul.

18

RICHARD DAVIS

You've got to make your contribution to whatever it is that you do, whether it be to your community, whether it be to society, or whether it's just to your little lad's football team.

G o to Liverpool, visit the fire service and meet Richard Davis, and you see how a public service right at the heart of the community can turn potential delinquents into good citizens and change young people's lives.

A few months ago, I attended a public services conference in London where Richard Davis brought an audience of public-service professionals alive with his story of how the fire service came to the aid of hard-to-help young people and helped them out of trouble. Hearing his story, I had to find out about how this firefighter and youth engagement officer was changing Merseyside. I found in Richard a shining example of the many remarkable individuals I have met who are working to maximise the positive impact public services can have within our communities.

For Richard, his commitment to his community is deeply rooted in his strong family background, which he speaks of with pride. 'You may have heard it all before, but the most important influence on me was my mum. She was a great believer in and campaigner for social justice. She came from a working-class family in Manchester and spent her entire life campaigning and working for poorer, socially disadvantaged people. She worked as a nursery nurse, but she could have, let's say, operated at a much higher level.

'Although she died a number of years ago, I think it was a philosophy that she imparted which contributes to my feeling that you've got to make a difference. You've got to make your contribution to whatever it is that you do, whether it be to your community, whether it be to society, or whether it's just to your little lad's football team. What I'm trying to do in Merseyside is show young people that there is an alternative, that they can come to us and feel part of something, that they can then have self-esteem and have status within a positive environment. The love, support and understanding I get from my wife Samantha and kids Annabel and Michael gives me the drive to help others who don't have such a happy, stable home life.'

Among the many unsung heroes who prompted me to write this book, I have found the dedication of those working in our public services particularly inspiring. Across the country, I have met individuals who are not only committing their professional lives to public service but also going far beyond the call of duty to give of themselves for the work they believe in. There can be few better illustrations of a willing commitment than the men and women of Britain's fire and rescue services. All day every day, 24/7, they are ready to answer the call and put themselves in danger to serve our communities. And as they seek to broaden the services' impact from creating safer communities to also creating stronger communities, community engagement is becoming a growing priority. With firefighters spending just 3 per cent of their time actually at a fire, the wider community role they can play is vital in our efforts to get more out of our public services. Richard's work on youth engagement at Merseyside Fire and Rescue is a powerful example of what can be achieved.

As a firefighter, Richard recognised that children and young people are too often involved in the negative elements of the work of the fire and rescue services, whether through deliberately lit fires, hoax calls or even violent attacks on firefighters. Now, he is trying to remedy this situation. 'We have a simple choice. We either get frustrated about the negative actions of some young people and stamp our feet and say, "Isn't the world awful?", which I don't happen to think it is by the way, or we get out there and do something about it. That's the core philosophy behind the work we have been doing with children and young people over recent years: we actually get out and work with young people, particularly the most challenging young people, the ones who present us with the most problems. The outcomes are reduced numbers of attacks and deliberate fires and hoax calls, but beyond that, people from the fire service demonstrate positive role models through our core values, teamwork and problem solving.'

The fire service is able to engage young people others might struggle to reach, because, as Richard explained, 'It's quite cool, quite sexy to young people. It's hands-on, it's practical, it's challenging, and young people thrive in the environment.' But above all, it is the fire service's can-do attitude that really speaks to them. 'When we face a problem in the fire service, we can't walk away from it. You don't see too many skeletons of cats in trees, and there aren't many fires that haven't been put out. We get things done, and we show we can get things done. I think that can-do, will-do philosophy translates really, really well when you work with young people, because they pick up on that.'

Richard got involved with the project initially by working with young people one day per week over a twelve-week course. 'In the morning, they'd have some classroom and team-building-type activities, and in the afternoon they'd come to me and I'd do a series of challenges with them – typical fire service type: here's a problem, here's a crisis, here's an emergency, you're dressed in full fire kit, now you've got to go and deal with it. You need leaders, you need teamwork, you need good communication, and they had to respond.' He and his team now run programmes in schools, programmes for young people excluded from school and a hugely successful programme for unemployed young people – over 80 per cent of whom go into full-time training, education or employment within ninety days of working with the Merseyside schemes.

Richard was aware of the need for analysis and evaluation of the work, but for him the real successes are measured in the one-to-one stories. 'It's about how many people move from where you start with them to where they end up. That's a figure, and that's great and that satisfies a lot of audit processes, but I think, probably, the high point really for me was the opportunity to come to Downing Street with a firefighter who joined me on that journey, and his name is Zico Haywood.

'He first came to my attention on one of my programmes. He was a nineteen-year-old young man who'd been out of work for four years before joining us. He'd had a very challenging background. He came from the care system. He'd had a very troubled upbringing to the extent where he'd witnessed one of his friends shoot one of his other friends. He'd witnessed people dying of crack cocaine overdoses, really horrendous. And he was trying to make a change in his life, trying to do something to improve it. I picked up on him. He's a very charismatic young man, and I presented him with a range of challenges that he's been successful in picking up, so much so that he has now moved on considerably. He got a job with me working with young people himself and has recently qualified as a firefighter serving the community of Merseyside.

'Zico was brought up on a road in Liverpool that's quite famous, Smithdown Road, and it really was like a story: "From Smithdown Road to Downing Street". You just couldn't have written it. It was a real achievement for him and, I guess, if I reflect on it, for me as well, for being able to help facilitate that transformation.'

Richard's enthusiasm for his work is so clear that it fills

everything he does with an infectious energy. And it is because he knows just how much he gets out of the work that he wants to make sure others can benefit from all it has to offer. 'I joined the fire service and found my true vocation. I absolutely loved it. The prospect of being paid to save people's lives and serve your community is a dream come true, really, and I want to make similar opportunities available for all our young people. I think one of the things that the fire service has at its core is the way in which it operates teams or, as we call them, watches. You're part of something, you wear a uniform and you can identify with something bigger than just yourself: they're positive things. One of the things the fire service can do for young people, who may often not necessarily come from strong communities or have strong social networks, is to provide an opportunity to feel part of something that contributes positively. I'm very often struck by the importance that young people give to wearing the football shirt: you support Liverpool or Manchester United. For me, being a Manchester United supporter in Liverpool can be a challenge! But it's important for people to feel part of something. One of the first things that a lot of young people want to do when they come and do some work with us is to wear the uniform and the badge of the fire service, and they wear it extremely proudly.

'I was looking at the weekend newspaper about the top twenty greatest speeches and it had that line in it from John F. Kennedy, that one about, "Ask not what your country can do for you, ask what you can do for your country." That's part of my philosophy, not just in terms of country but in everything that I do. I want to put in the maximum. I try to impart that into everything that I do and all the people that I work with, particularly young people.'

An important influence for Richard is the leadership of his local fire and rescue service, and he was keen that I understood the lessons that could be learnt across the public services from what they had achieved. 'Merseyside began doing this kind of community work in 1999, years before it became expected. And I believe that's one of the reasons that we're the highest-performing fire authority, because we believe in strong communities. If it wasn't for the leadership having the vision and bravery to support the work that we do with children and young people, none of it would happen. It does require an enormous amount of bravery, because the people we work with are high risk. But there is a guiding hand, a vision that they have got of broadening the ambition, celebrating innovation and change, and – what's that horrendous expression? – pushing the envelope. To be perfectly honest with you, all that my role has been is to try and work in an organisation that allows that innovation to happen. Dare to fail, that's the thing. I think we should celebrate innovation. Support it. Have public services operating in a climate that supports innovation as opposed to a climate of fear, I guess.

'When you are working with some very vulnerable young people, if you get things wrong, it can have some pretty catastrophic consequences. Part of the can-do philosophy is the idea that you know where the problems are and it's very often not difficult to come up with the solutions. Just get on with it. Just do it. Not, "Let's form another quality circle, or another focus group, or another committee." We know where the kids are hanging out. We know there is a problem in a certain part of town; well, go and do something.

'One prime example of that was when we had some young people in a part of Merseyside who were causing us some problems on a Friday and Saturday night. We went and spoke to them and said, "What do you want to do?" They were quite literally climbing all over some of the public buildings in the area and causing problems, not just to us but to the people who owned the buildings, to the police and the people who lived in that community. We said, "Well, OK, there isn't anything to do round here, tell us what you want to do." They were obviously into climbing and they said, "Well, we want to do some climbing." I said, "All right then, we'll put a climbing wall in the fire station." So we built a climbing wall, and the young people maintain it, they work there and they come and run sessions now for other young people. So, we knew where the problem was, talked to the people and got on with it.'

Richard's passionate commitment to the work he does goes beyond simply providing a first-class public service: he has big ambitions for the role the fire service could come to play within communities. 'A lot of people, in my opinion, wrongly hark back to the days of national service: national service, shiny boots, shiny mind and all that. I've got a vision of the fire service being like a national service for young people, in a voluntary capacity where young people can work with the fire service like they do with us in Merseyside, experiencing our core values of teamwork, respect, raising self-esteem, achieving something together and challenging yourself within a very positive framework. It's about saving people's lives and reducing risks to the community. What work can you do in your community?'

Public servants like Richard are not simply 'doing their job'. They are the linchpins at the very centre of our communities, bringing people together, touching so many of our lives in different ways and helping each of us feel safer and more secure. We must never take for granted their commitment, for it will form the very foundations of the good society.

PATHFINDERS

Voluntary action has always had the power to bring new challenges to public attention. And British voluntary action has often led the world, being more innovative, more forward looking, more responsive to new needs than anywhere else. Long before government took notice, individuals and voluntary associations saw wrongs that had to be righted: from organisations to help the homeless, feed the hungry and care for the sick; from supporting refugees or the victims of abuse to rehabilitating offenders and addicts; from playgroups and online networks to support parents and carers to intergenerational volunteer initiatives to tackle isolation among the elderly.

In this we are all the beneficiaries of past generations: of a British tradition of social innovation stretching from Robert Owen, William Morris, Florence Nightingale, Edwin Chadwick and Joseph Rowntree to the rise of cooperatives, trade unions and civic pioneers, and, in the post-war years, organisations from the Open University to the Consumers' Association.

The challenge for every era is to show whether it possesses the creative talent and imagination to solve its new problems. And today I am able to see some of the world's most innovative people once more reaching out in new areas. In our generation we have seen the remarkable rise of the hospice movement and Aids charities, the playgroup movement and now the social technology network, third-age societies and the boom in social enterprise.

Often innovative individuals and voluntary groups can do more: take risks, try things out, work informally, do things differently, break new ground, cross new frontiers and meet new needs. Through their capacity for innovation, and untrammelled by bureaucracy, volunteers and voluntary organisations often change the way we see things and do things. And again and again they show that people have the capacity to remake their own lives.

Such innovation is all the more important because we live in a period of perhaps the most rapid social change in our history. The pace of change now demands constant innovation. New challenges need rapid responses and creative answers; and mass population movement and global conflict, changing demographics and family structures, new trends in crime and addiction, and the changing needs of our young people all present new challenges. Indeed, some of the biggest problems we face are ones that arise from our greater interdependence – from the environment to communities under pressure of change – and it is often the people closest to these changes who are able to respond most quickly and effectively.

We all acknowledge – as I do in my introduction – that some of the traditional forms of association are declining in memberships. But anyone who equates this change with an overall decline in voluntary activity or even a collapse of community should take a minute to consider the manifold and inspiring new forms of social participation that I have witnessed and the creative thinking I have seen applied to seemingly intractable problems.

This section contains the stories of these pathfinders: innovators pioneering new forms of social action or new solutions to key challenges – the Internet developer pioneering new mechanisms of democratic engagement, and the social entrepreneurs using business models to invest in young people and in the environment; the women in London who have developed new approaches to supporting children's emotional needs, and the needs of the sickest children and their families; the youth workers in Preston and the Isle of Skye pioneering new approaches to engaging some of the hardest to reach and realising in them potential they never knew they had; the men harnessing the transformative power of the arts by bringing ballet to a deprived estate and opera to the homeless; the woman who has led new efforts to maintain family bonds between prisoners and their children; the frontline worker who has helped to develop a new form of intensive intervention with troubled families; and the child psychologist who has effectively eradicated illiteracy in his region of Scotland.

These are just a few of the many pioneers who are making efforts and taking risks to do things as they have never been done before in order to find ever more effective ways to help people, bring people together and tackle new challenges. They are helping to shape the future of our communities and our public services. We must learn the lessons from their beginnings, for they are the pathfinders towards a better society.

19

TOM STEINBERG

We particularly aim to serve people who may be very dependent on the state but who are not very literate about how to get what they need out of it.

Talk to Tom Steinberg and every second sentence offers you a new idea about technology, communications, citizenship and, most of all, democratic engagement.

I wanted to talk to Tom because he is the founder of mySociety, a social enterprise project that is leading the way in exploring how technology can reinvigorate democratic engagement. Tom and his team are the creators of pioneering sites such as TheyWorkForYou, WriteToThem and PledgeBank. As Tom explained to me, mySociety has two missions: to build websites that give citizens simple tools to communicate their concern to their elected representatives, and to demonstrate to both the voluntary and the public sector how technology can be put to work to help people.

Tom explained one of his recent projects, Neighbourhood Fix-It, which combines both these objectives. 'It's simply about getting stuff in your neighbourhood fixed,' he explains. 'On the website, you get a map of your local area, you stick a pin in the map and say there is a problem here. The site works out which council area you're in, because you might not know, and it sends your report to where it needs to go.'

Too often, Tom argues, services and democracy are treated as two separate things. As this project demonstrates, engaging people in discussions about the provision of local services as they engage with service delivery is a practical demonstration of grass-roots democracy. 'What it's really about is a deeper agenda, opening up the process by which local problems get solved and fixed. Let's just take a really simple piece of service delivery, like fixing something on the street. Why can't people have discussions about it in the process of fixing it? If we make people have discussions only in political places, if we say, "Well, you get your bins fixed and then you go somewhere else to have a discussion about why your bins were broken in the first place", they won't do the second one. We exist to help the council fix your problem, but we're going to encourage you right then and there, in that act of reporting, to create a dialogue about what's going on.'

As Neighbourhood Fix-It shows, the incredible pace of technological advance is changing the ways we interact and communicate, the ways we organise ourselves and form communities, the ways we participate, make decisions and express ourselves. While some might worry that technology can threaten our traditional modes of social interaction, for a new generation of social activists like Tom, communications technologies are an invaluable tool in the pursuit of a more connected, more participative and even more caring social world.

Tom explained how mySociety began. 'I always had a bit of a technical background and an interest in the Internet. I was a civil servant, and I realised that the Government was putting an awful lot of stuff online, but it wasn't doing anything very new, and, crucially, it wasn't doing things that were about citizens and government agencies getting together. They were making it possible to renew your passport online, for example. Same process, no democracy, just service delivery.'

In 2003, Tom became involved with the volunteer community that had already established some websites to connect local people to their elected representatives. 'One of the things that was originally built by volunteers, and which inspired me and the community to build an organisation, is called WriteToThem. This website does the simplest of things. You put in your postcode and it tells you who your elected representatives are, then you can contact them. That doesn't seem glamorous until you realise that 60 per cent of people don't know who their Member of Parliament is and far more people don't know who their councillor is, or even that they have a councillor or an MEP.

'That service has delivered just under 90,000 messages, but, crucially, half of those people told us that they had never written to a politician before in their lives. We also know that more people from the most deprived fifth of wards used it than the least deprived fifth. It managed to connect several tens of thousands of people who never engaged in politics for any reason ever before directly with their policy makers, their representatives.'

As Tom explained, a vital part of the role of mySociety is to open up a discussion about what constitutes democratic engagement. 'These are not tools for "political junkies". We are at exactly the opposite end of the scale. We particularly aim to serve people who may be very dependent on the state but who are not very literate about how to get what they need out of it.'

While many people bemoan a perceived political apathy amongst much of the public, Tom and his team refuse to accept that this is true. 'I think people in our organisation care that we live in a democracy, and they care when it feels like it could be done better or when it feels like it's just being overtaken by events. When it feels like everything else in life is accelerating and responding to people's desires and needs. Democracy really means something to people in this modern age, nobody wants it to go away.'

Alongside practical web-based mechanisms for connecting citizens to their elected representatives, Tom believes that mySociety, as a voluntary-sector organisation, can demonstrate innovative systems in practice, providing evidence for public-sector agencies to adopt and implement new technologies and new ways of working. 'Government needs examples to learn from, because they have a duty to be risk-averse, and there's nothing wrong with that. We don't want them throwing all our money away, but they need people to copy. We believe we can build things ourselves that will really help members of the public straightaway: direct benefits that help people and make us feel good about running this organisation. But we can also build things that people in the public sector will see and say, "Why don't we have one of them? Can't we make our thing work like that?"'

Tom is a leading light amongst an emerging movement of inspiring innovators who are developing new mechanisms for deliberative democracy. While his websites are achieving remarkable success, he explained that actions such as signing a petition or contacting your MP are just the first stage of engagement. The real challenge now is to develop ways in which we encourage people who take these first small steps of engagement to move into deeper levels of democratic participation and to get involved in genuine public debate.

Tom's successes in boosting democratic engagement include the No. 10 Downing Street e-petition site he created, which has received more than two and a half million signatures. But it is not only democracy that interests him. Tom is keen on all other ways in which technology can help people to get together and organise things that matter to them. The PledgeBank website, for example, allows people to create a pledge, along the lines of, 'I'll do something, but only if other people will pledge to do the same thing.' This can be from the very small scale, such as running a street party, to larger shared ventures. 'It was great when we saw campaigners set up the Open Rights group using our website at PledgeBank. Lots of these people cared about the same issues, it almost doesn't matter what those issues are, but they've never had the funding to build an organisation. They set up a pledge that said, "I will set up a standing order of £5 a month to establish and maintain this organisation, but only if 1,000 other people will also set up a standing order", and they got it. They didn't get all of their 1,000, but they got enough so there is an organisation, it has staff, it's active and it's out there campaigning on Internet privacy and censorship. They just created a civil-society organisation that wouldn't have existed otherwise, because they set up and pledged on the PledgeBank site. It's full of great examples like that.

'Very recently we got some pictures from India of a new library that's been set up by people who signed a big pledge and said, "I will donate money or donate books to support a new library, but only if 1,000 other people will." We watched them push and push for many months, and they got their 1,000 people. When you get the photos of the finished library, it's just an amazing feeling.'

Utilising new technologies for pro-social benefit is helping us to do new things together, and helping us to do the things we have always done, but do them better, quicker and more effectively. 'It's not rocket science this Internet stuff,' said Tom. 'It's not just about waving your hands and talking about how the world is changing. Really simple benefits enable people to connect, and we hear the results: for example, "I had no idea the council would ever do anything, but they're outside my window right now fixing the paving slabs." That's the nature of the Internet: if you make something fairly simple, it can, if you are lucky, benefit loads of people, meaning that the ratio of rewards to investment is brilliant. I can't think of another way in which three or four paid people could help many thousands of people.'

20

KATE KING

*The young people, they're the generation of tomorrow.
They need to have the ability to shape their lives and
they need to do that for themselves.*

T he stories I tell in this book originated in many different ways. Some people were motivated by personal experiences in their lives, others by seeing a need they wanted to fill or an injustice they wanted to put right. But only one story began with a dream.

One night in 1995, Kate King dreamt up what is now called the Dreamscheme. It came to her as an idea and an almost fully formed plan: a new way of working with the young people on the Flower Estate in Sheffield where she was living.

Kate had been a foster carer, and this helped to shape her views on working with young people. 'I'd just become so passionate. The negative attitude towards young people had been growing, so I wanted to find ways to encourage a positive attitude instead. My one word for it is affirmation. Lots of young people spend incredibly small amounts of time in the company of adults who approve of them. They get approval from their peers, but in school, on the streets, wherever, they are disapproved of. They spend very little time in the company of adults who give them back some affirmation, some approval on a one-to-one basis.'

Kate was driven by these concerns and inspired by a strong personal faith. And so, in much the same way as she dreamt it, Dreamscheme became a reality. It is a very straightforward plan. Young people are encouraged to do local work projects and they gain points for each hour worked. The points have a value and can be spent by the young people going on trips of their choice. The last bit of the dream was that the money to make all of this happen would come from local businesses.

The first Dreamscheme was established in 1995, working with around 100 eleven to eighteen year olds from the Flower Estate. Kate worked full time setting up and running the project, although it was three years before she took any salary. 'We got to know all the young people and got to understand what the real issues are for those living in such places.' In 1999, the initial Dreamscheme began to operate in partnership with many of the large housing associations, setting up local versions of the original scheme in different parts of the country. 'Housing associations were expected to address the issues of young people on their estates. When they ask their residents about their key concerns, obviously nuisance comes high up the list, but they don't have the resources to respond. The Dreamscheme is an ideal vehicle, because it doesn't require the building of new youth centres; it's simply an activity that they can implement.'

The Dreamscheme model has now been applied across the UK and beyond. Each local group is unique and dependent on the skills of the adults involved, and there is an almost limitless range of work projects: they can be environmental, social, creative, enterprising or relate to personal development. 'In one project, a small group of teenagers made a garden bench for the people in the local residential home for the elderly. They made it in the morning, took it round in the afternoon and had their photo taken with everybody sitting on it. A lot of the work goes back to some older-fashioned skills that we seem to be losing: cooking, baking, gardening – very basic. The kids get their points for doing it and get to meet the people they live alongside; in the process, they get approval.'

Kate was clear about the powerful impact that the Dreamscheme can have on individual young lives, but when asked about its overall significance, she would only say modestly, 'Oh, it's far too soon to tell. We've only been going ten years!' She did, however, reflect on some of the successes of the Dreamscheme project: 'Having kids knock on the door and say, "Have you got some work for us today?"; while working in the kitchen making bread, young people themselves come out with things like, "You learn respect here, don't you?"; old people sending birthday cards to the young people on the estate who used to be terrorising it . . . I see social capital being built instead of social terror. I see creativity instead of destruction.'

Kate's emphasis on affirming the positive and reinforcing and rewarding actions that are socially useful is a powerful theme that runs through the core of the work. 'We've invented the word "PROSBO": "Pro-Social Behaviour Options". Kids go around with letters telling them that they've been awarded a PROSBO, so they've got PROSBOs instead of ASBOs. I walked into a very successful, noteworthy youth centre, and there were two noticeboards: one labelled "Drugs" and the other labelled "Antisocial Behaviour". The little coffee bar was over by the drugs noticeboard, so I went and collected my coffee, and I said with a smile, "What drugs have you got for sale today?" And they said, "Whoa, there's none on sale."

'"I thought it was a noticeboard for drugs," I said. "Why haven't you got the brilliant things that the kids have done this week on one board and all of the positive brilliant things that the kids could do next week on the other board? What difference would that make if they came in one day and the antisocial board had gone, the drugs board had gone, and their PROSBO certificate was there instead and their PROSBO T-shirts were waiting to be printed?" What effect does it have on young people if they're constantly blighted with how many of them have got ASBOs? It feeds the fear of crime. It feeds the fear of young people. It's not so long ago that young people used to walk in slight fear of older people, and we've managed to reverse that so that the old people are now far too often afraid of young people. If I can contribute to a change in paradigm, a change of perspective from the negative attitude we have towards young people, then it's worth walking the planet.'

Kate's passion was clear in all the stories she wanted to tell me, all the individuals whose lives she had touched and who in turn had clearly touched her own. 'I can tell you of the kids that have been a Dreamscheme young person and they are now qualified youth workers. I can tell you about young people that have done Dreamscheme and are at university. I can tell you about a kid in Salford who was so made up with his first Dreamscheme little certificate that he said, "I won't have to sell *The Big Issue* now." The rungs on the ladder start lower down.'

Kate's inspiring example has sparked similar projects across the world. An Internet search even turned up a project in the foothills of Kilimanjaro, where volunteers had started a Dreamscheme helping with gardening projects and growing vegetables. A chance meeting at a Birmingham training event led to Kate working with communities in Kampala and Jinja in Uganda, establishing versions of the Dreamscheme there. 'In some ways, the top line of what we do in Uganda is we export fun. It would be great to be known for exporting fun to Uganda!' And across the world, Dreamscheme is not only helping young people but also helping to bring them together. 'I had a wonderful time in Northern Ireland over Easter just working on a garden in Belfast with young people and having the privilege of being able to inspire them and being well received as well. So in Northern Ireland, young people are delighted that Catholics and Protestants can work together. The Dreamscheme in Uganda has got Muslims and Christians on the committee. I don't know where Dreamscheme will go.'

Like all organisations, there have been some difficult times. 'It's hard when local groups fail to get continued funding, or the adults, for very good reasons, just can't carry on and the kids don't have a Dreamscheme in the end. That's tough, facing that one. You know the good stuff that's potentially going to happen to the kids, and you want to wave a magic wand, but you can't.'

Kate talked about how, in overcoming the difficulties, she draws on her Christian faith for personal support. 'The Dreamscheme is a registered charity: it works with housing associations and is a secular, good-quality deliverer, offering training, advice and support to anybody who wants to do Dreamscheme. But my personal story is that I am guided by God and supported by what I believe, and I have trust and faith.'

When we talked about what she had learnt through all her work, Kate had a very clear message to anyone thinking about getting involved in their community. 'Avoid complexity. Seek simplicity. Dreamscheme is extremely practical; it isn't theoretical and it isn't abstract. If you want to make a difference to something, then you actually have to do something. You have to stop thinking about it, theorising and planning; you actually have to do it. That's what I've personally done quite a few times. I've done it and then thought afterwards, "What on earth did I do? Has it worked?" Live more adventurously. If you want to inspire, you have to live the whole of your life as an adventure. I think we're due for a social revolution, but we'd do the risk assessment first.

'I don't actually believe that social change which delivers social capital can come from the top down. My passion and my commitment, my full-time occupation, is building the relationships on the ground so that the grass roots are the source of the power for change. The young people, they're the generation of tomorrow. They need to have the ability to shape their lives and they need to do that for themselves. It's great watching kids have fun: it's like a cloud has lifted. We're creating too many clouds over their lives. They are the future generation, and they need to have fun. Risk aversion and materialism both collude to minimise what you are meant to be doing in childhood: collecting stories for your own grandchildren.'

Politicians and academics and practitioners can spend a long time trying to understand social challenges, trying to define causes and design solutions, trying to gather evidence and test theories. But as I have learnt over the years, it is often a very simple idea, carried out with love and with care that can actually make the most difference. And from Kate King I learnt the value of one simple idea in particular: the power of fun to lift us up.

21

MATT PEACOCK

I feel that we act as a community – a neighbourhood –
for a group of people who are not listened to enough.

Think back to the early 1990s, shortly after Mrs Thatcher
had announced that there was 'no such thing as society',
and remember how an MP triggered national outrage by saying
ironically that he knew all about the homeless: they were the
people 'you step over on your way out of the opera'.

This remark remained with Matt Peacock for years and
sparked an idea that was to change his life and give us one of
the most innovative charities of this decade.

Matt had his first experience of London life in his twenties
and was shocked at the number of people sleeping rough on
the streets, apparently with no one to turn to. 'I felt helpless. I
couldn't offer any kind of friendship or support, and the public
seemed to have zero tolerance of them, portraying them all as
drug users or alcoholics. I could see that wasn't the case – the
situation was much more complicated than that – but I felt
there was nothing I could do. I vented my frustration in the
only way I could, by complaining about it to my friends, until
one day one of my flatmates snapped and asked why didn't I
stop whingeing and do something about it. Of course he was
right: it's not enough to feel strongly about an issue, it's what
you do about it that's important.'

Matt was a professional arts worker when he began
volunteering in a homeless centre in Westminster, and eventually

became a fully trained frontline support worker. 'The residents at the shelter told me that, while they felt quite supported in all kinds of practical ways, they felt there was a problem with the public not respecting them and having misconceptions about them – that there was a stigma attached to being homeless. There was very little to do that was creative or interesting in the homeless centres or in the homeless sector in general. They wanted a project where they could show the public what they could do. So we had the idea of taking that remark about homeless people outside the opera house and turning it on its head by having the homeless people from the hostel help to create an opera production, which we staged in the year 2000 in the Linbury Studio Theatre at the Royal Opera House.

'There were some professional performers involved. And because it was a children's opera, there were some kids from the local school. And the people from the homeless shelter wanted to be involved but by working backstage: putting together sets, working on costumes and design, that kind of thing. None of them actually performed, but at the end, everyone took to the stage and was applauded by a packed house. I'm still in touch with one of the guys who was involved who said that moment played a large part in helping him put his life back in order. They felt they were being taken seriously, and at a time when there was a lot of debate in the media about homelessness, we got some positive coverage.'

Then, as now, there was a perception that homelessness was about rough sleeping, although, in fact, rough sleepers account for a very small percentage of the homeless people in the country. Matt explained, 'It is very important for the public to recognise that homelessness is much more than rough sleeping. It is very easy for people to become homeless or have housing problems, and there are lots of people out there who are in very vulnerable circumstances. They're not visible, they're not begging in the street; they're a group you don't really get to hear about, and they are the people that organisations like mine support.'

Matt's organisation is Streetwise Opera, which he set up two years after that show in the Linbury Studio Theatre with two main aims: first, to educate the public with some clear and positive messages about homeless people; and, second, to offer homeless people a chance to rebuild their self-esteem and confidence through creative involvement with opera. Streetwise Opera has a regular weekly programme of workshops, trips to the theatre, performances and work placements. The work is based at nine centres throughout Britain, with some in America, and they have an invitation to stage a show at Sydney Opera House in a couple of years' time. Its productions have been staged in locations including Westminster Abbey and West End theatres, but the core of the project is Streetwise Live, a programme of 500 workshops a year, all working directly with homeless and ex-homeless people, which are based in day centres, homeless centres and hostels.

Matt explained, 'We have very clear aims about using the work to support what is done in the homeless centres by offering personal development for the participants. It is about confidence, self-esteem, building social networks, and encouraging creativity. Working with some specialists, we have just developed a new evaluation system which shows clearly that if you build confidence and self-esteem it has a positive impact on people's lives. That comes across in people getting back in touch with friends and family, increasing their employability and enjoying more independent living, and we have done research which demonstrates that when people are working on productions, when they have that positive engagement with work on a project, it has a direct and positive impact on their lives: for example, it reduces their alcohol consumption and reduces the likelihood of their self-harming.'

Matt's work is driven by a strong belief in the potential of every individual and an awareness that when you give people a chance to realise that potential, they can achieve what neither they, nor anyone else, might have expected they could. 'We want participants to feel that they can succeed even when everyone else has low expectations of them. Perhaps they have always felt that they are a bit of a problem and a drain on society. We give them a platform on which to celebrate; we let them show the public what they can do. The impact of that process is obvious when you see it. It's compelling to witness the transformation. One of my motivations to keep going is when I hear people say that if only they had had this opportunity when they were younger, maybe their lives could have turned out differently. I happen to feel strongly about homelessness, which is why I worked in a centre as a volunteer and then as a member of staff. And the opportunity arose for us to fill a gap. I feel that we act as a community – a neighbourhood – for a group of people who are not listened to enough.'

Streetwise Opera has a completely open-door policy. There are no auditions. The workshops are open to anyone who wants to come and are closely integrated with the day-to-day work of the homeless centres where they take place. The organisation has three members of staff based in London and a pool of twenty-five trained workshop leaders. Like many small arts organisations, it receives almost no core funding, relying on a trickle of project funds from the Arts Council of England, trusts, foundations and some local authorities.

Through a range of different activities, Matt and his team seek to provide development opportunities for homeless people and to bring the realities of homelessness to the public. As well as workshops and performances, each year they run hundreds of work-placement days for homeless people in organisations like the Royal Opera House, the Royal Albert Hall, Nottingham Playhouse and the Sage at Gateshead. And once a year there is a big show, which is a key element in the Streetwise commitment to educate the public.

Matt explained, 'The process is to bring in a team of experts and create a show that is highly professional, but also to invite the homeless participants to join that process. The professional singers and the creative team are bringing their expertise; the homeless participants are bringing their commitment and their experience. So what you see is a polished performance but it includes a group of homeless and ex-homeless people, and it is put together by means of workshops in the homeless centres. Everyone works and rehearses to devise the show together. All the shows have received at least four stars in the broadsheet papers. We have had a couple of big documentaries on radio and television, and we also do smaller performances at anything from the Labour Party conference to shows for homeless charities and small festivals.

'There's always been a stigma around opera, but we use that to our advantage. It has always been a case of creating something that is going to be interesting for the media to grasp hold of. It sort of validates what we do. When we get a whole page in the *New York Times*, when we get asked to be on the *Today Programme* or make a documentary, it helps to promote positive attitudes about homelessness. And, if you think that whenever you look in a newspaper and read about homelessness it tends to be a negative story, just the fact that we are doing this and promoting positive attitudes is very powerful – and quite unique.'

Formerly a professional in the music business, Matt is very aware of the power of the arts to touch people's lives, and he continually stresses the impact of the arts on the Streetwise participants. 'It is not the case that everyone wants a job out of it or even that everyone wants to get housing out of it. It is much more subtle than that. It is about giving people back their self-respect, allowing them to enjoy more independent living and making them look forward to getting up the next day. Someone at our last show was a very long-term alcohol user. He had lost touch with his family and friends, who had almost disowned him, but he helped backstage at the Sage in Gateshead. Through that he was able to invite his family along, and so he got back in touch with them, told them he was doing something positive, and he was able to see his daughter for the first time in seven years and meet his granddaughter for the first time. We had another guy who was the victim of a very serious mugging and spent something like six months in hospital. He became homeless after that and his confidence was very low, but he engaged with what we had to offer and worked on one of our shows. We put him in a work placement at the Royal Albert Hall, where he got a job, and he came out of depression that way.'

For many of Streetwise's participants, who may have very complex needs, suffer from serious mental illness or have learning difficulties, measuring impact only against outcomes such as finding a job doesn't tell the full story of what they have gained. So Matt has been determined to find a way of evaluating what Streetwise really achieves. The motivation is very practical. 'You have to be very realistic about setting up something new. You need to be able to demonstrate that you are needed, because if you're not needed you won't get funding. You have to be able to prove the benefit of your work. Everyone who has been part of our workshops has said more or less the same thing: that they have benefited in six ways – in confidence, enjoyment, self-esteem, the ability to make new friends, skills and creativity. Out of that feedback we developed what we called an "Evaluation Tree", so that we can calculate the percentage increase in confidence or social networking that results from a project. That evaluation system is now used by the homeless sector to demonstrate to the Government the value of the arts in the support system for homeless people.'

Matt is passionate about the way the arts can help to transform the whole of a person. He has found imaginative and innovative ways to challenge public assumptions about homelessness and homeless people, and to turn stigma into education and celebration. And, when experience of homelessness, and all the multiple needs and difficulties which sit alongside homelessness, can rob a person of their self-esteem, their confidence, their sense of belonging and identity, he has worked to give some of the most vulnerable people in our society a way to feel like themselves again, a way to imagine new possibilities, and a way to feel part of a community.

Matt is passionately committed to the idea that the arts are not just some attractive but inessential add-on in the process of changing the future for homeless people; they can be the driver of the whole process. 'I feel that the work we do has come from a recognised need. These people have been in the background. Putting them in the spotlight, literally, is all the motivation that we and they need. And we can prove it works!'

22

PAT BEATTIE

The difference is that we don't go away. We stay
around and we stay around for a long time. There's no
limit to the length of time that we work with families.

G o to Dundee, visit a standard 1960s council-house
block in an ordinary estate, knock on the door of the
Dundee Families Project as I did, and you will find, behind
the ordinary exterior, a pioneering and life-changing project at
work: families best known for persistent antisocial behaviour
and for repeat evictions turning their lives around. The starting
point for these families is not tea and sympathy but a contract:
twenty-four-hour-a-day, seven-day-a-week support, but only if
they sign up to a day-by-day plan of action to change their
behaviour. And as Pat Beattie, who has been part of the project
since its inception, explained to me, they have achieved results
that many others had thought impossible.

Pat's involvement began when she herself was worried about
what might happen to her teenage daughter. 'I went back to
college as a mature student when my own children grew up. I
was bored being a cook and needed some other challenges in
my life, so I decided to go back to university and study home
economics, health and social education. Then, in my first
year there, my husband was diagnosed with leukaemia and
died within the year. It had a real impact on all of our lives,
obviously, but it particularly affected my youngest daughter:
her life totally changed. What we went through made me realise

that there are a lot of people out there in similar situations.

'I was lucky. I didn't lose my house and didn't get into drugs. But I think I had an understanding of the impact on families, the kind of dysfunction that can result from something like a death in the family. So I really stuck in at college and managed to get through. Just as I was coming to the end of my time at university, the project was opening. So the course that I had done, and the personal experience that I had been through that time, led me into this line of work.'

The Dundee Families Project was initiated by the city council in Dundee, who worked with NCH, the children's charity, to implement it. They realised that evicting families because of their antisocial behaviour was no solution but simply moved the problem elsewhere and compounded the difficulties, particularly for children who were already unsettled. The project aimed to promote stability, reduce homelessness and improve quality of life, particularly for children whose lives were disrupted as a result of their parents' behaviour. A residential unit was created to house up to three families at any one time. This unit provides self-contained flats where intensive support is offered twenty-four hours a day to help families who display the most difficult antisocial behaviour. The unit has been running successfully for ten years now, but it wasn't an easy project to get off the ground, with local press voicing considerable opposition before it opened.

Pat, on the staff team from the beginning, recalled those first days. 'Day one was 12 August 1996 at 9.30 in the morning. I remember it very well: it was very exciting. Prior to that there had been a huge hullabaloo about the project opening in Dundee. It had been in the newspapers for months: "Sin Bin to Open", it was called "Colditz" and a whole host of other things. So showing up on the first day was quite nerve-wracking. The whole staff team started together.'

But rather than deterring her, it was this negative press coverage that initially made Pat determined to work on the project. 'I read all the stuff that was in the paper. I had just finished college after returning as a mature student, and it was the type of work that I wanted to do. I was very keen to work with families, and because it had been so high profile in the local papers, I knew that it was coming, so, basically, I was just waiting for the job advert in the paper. It was something so new and so different. It wasn't a way that anybody was working up until that point. This seemed such a new concept: that I could be working across all the disciplines and working with the whole family, not just with individuals within that family. That didn't happen before. You either worked with the adults or you worked with the children, and never the twain shall meet.'

Referrals to the project come for a number of different reasons, but whatever the behaviour patterns, intensive support is put in place, including parenting skills, anger management and life-skills support such as basic cooking and household budgeting. Alcohol and drugs counselling is also offered to those who would benefit from it. 'If the family are willing to work with the project, we undertake a thorough assessment that will give us the information that we need to put into the support plan and give us the focus of the work that we would be undertaking with the family. The support plans that we prepare with families are multi-agency. We work with any other agencies that are assisting the family; we don't operate in isolation. This ensures that the families are getting the best service that they can possibly get.

'I couldn't say that there's an actual typical family because there just isn't one,' explained Pat. 'Increasingly, there are higher numbers with parental drug and alcohol misuse. We've had more families experiencing mental-health difficulties and parental learning difficulties as well. It's very wide ranging. We need a family to acknowledge that there is a problem and to work towards dealing with that problem. Every new family that you meet poses a different challenge. They may come with the same presenting problems, but there are different individuals within every family, so you deal with each case differently. Every day there is something new; every day you have to learn something different. I think you learn a lot about yourself as you go along.'

The success of the Dundee Families Project's approach lies in the intensity of support on offer combined with the explicit expectation of behaviour change. Families know that there is someone on hand ready to give them the time and support they need whenever they need it. But they also know that a lot is expected of them: they are expected to make changes in their lives, and they have to keep to their side of the deal. 'A lot of the families that we've worked with have had people coming in and out of their lives for a long time. They come in and they read the riot act or they tell them to do this, that and the next thing, and then they go away. The difference is that we don't go away. We stay around and we stay around for a long time. There's no limit to the length of time that we work with families. Nobody says that after a year the funding runs out and we won't be back. We're there. We challenge regularly. But we're also there to support the family and stand up for them when it's required. We'll go in and battle to get children back into school. We'll argue with the education authorities. We'll battle with the health services to get the support in for families that they need. Families recognise that: they know that whilst you can be quite hard with them, you're also there to support them.

'It is a clear balance between challenge and support. When families first start working with us, it's more challenge, probably, than support. Because we are trying to get them into a pattern of life, into a lifestyle that's going to be suitable for them and help their children move on. But it's also about building up the one-to-one relationship of trust. Families need to know that you are going to be there for them, regardless of what they do. We're not going to go away. They will try to shock you sometimes. They swear at you and curse at you and threaten you. But we don't go away. And I think they can then understand why we demand the commitment from them to move forward.'

When I visited Dundee to see the family intervention at work, I was struck by how the project's success was rooted in the relationship that is built up between staff like Pat and the families they work with. I met a twenty-six-year-old single parent with two children, let's call her 'Lisa'. For ten years, Lisa had been, in her own words, 'off the rails'. Her lifestyle was chaotic, and after being evicted from her flat, she was at the point of losing her children into care when she was referred to the project. The 'tough love' message to her was clear: 'sign up to change or lose your children'. She signed a support plan, which required her to do specific things, and in return she would get access to targeted services. Most importantly, she received one-to-one support, 24/7, if she was in difficulty. She had to agree that if certain people came to see her at home they would not be given admission. A new discipline was imposed, but she was given the support to chase the old damaging influences out of her life. Now Lisa is taking pride in her children and is planning a career as a care worker. She is about to go to college and has undertaken a parenting course at her first child's school. Lisa said to me that what she received from her mentors was the encouragement, support, advice and instruction that she should have received from her parents. For Lisa, and for her two children, the cycle is broken.

One of the most important lessons that I have learnt from the stories I tell in this book is that quick fixes don't change lives, and quick solutions can become undone just as quickly. To really make a difference to someone whose life has taken a difficult turn requires patience and persistence. Being there for someone, being in it for the long haul, can be frustrating and thankless, but it is often the only thing that works. And, simple as it sounds, it really can work.

Pat has now moved on from the NCH Dundee Families Project to lead a new project in Aberdeen, replicating the success she had in Dundee. As she works to build upon the lessons she has learnt, she is inspired by each of the families whose lives have been transformed through the project she helped initiate more than ten years ago. 'I always think back to the very first family that I worked with. Mum had mental-health issues that hadn't been diagnosed. When I finished working with her after about three or four years, she went to college, got qualifications and is managing her life. She got back in touch with family that she had lost contact with, the children were attending school regularly, and she was happy. When we stopped working with her, she was a happy woman. Whereas when I first started working with her, she was distraught, very anxious. It was just a wonderful experience to see how she'd come on and how her children had come on as well. It was fantastic, and I think that was the case with most of the families I have worked with. I have always felt that I was leaving them in a better place than they were when they started off.'

23

BENITA REFSON

If we have a solid early years' experience then we have the resilience and the capacity to cope with whatever life dishes out.

According to the Mental Health Foundation, one in five young people will experience a mental-health problem over the course of a year. That imposes a huge burden on parents, schools and communities, but most importantly it imposes a terrible toll on the children themselves, whether this is expressed in antisocial behaviour or, as it commonly is, in depression, withdrawal and self-harming. Many children find themselves in school, unable to cope, unable to benefit, unable to contribute and, most of all, feeling there is no one they can talk to.

Benita Refson saw the problem and decided to do something about it. And the result is The Place2Be, an innovative, growing charity that gives children in primary schools a place where they can express their feelings through talking, creative work and play. When I talked to Benita about what drove her forward, she explained that her motivation to create the organisation grew out of her experiences as a counsellor and as a parent.

Working with students at University College London and with adolescents at the Wandsworth Youth Agency in south London, Benita saw something particularly challenging in the issues presented by both groups of young people. The university students were focused on getting their degrees and getting on;

the young people at the Wandsworth Youth Agency were lost, depressed, often resorting to crime. 'But they were both quite difficult groups to engage with. And I was continually thinking that if only I had had the chance to work with them at a younger age, because the way they were experiencing distress as young adults was very much to do with unresolved issues from when they were children. Metaphorically, it is like someone falling down and scraping their knee: if the wound is treated then it is never more than a superficial cut, but if it is ignored it can fester and leave a scar.

'As a parent I was interested in providing my children with the opportunity to talk. When they were very young, we used to have what I called DCs – deep conversations – and I think being able to talk openly about how you feel is essential to our emotional well-being. I genuinely believe that being there for children is really, really important. If we have a solid early years' experience then we have the resilience and the capacity to cope with whatever life dishes out. But if you don't have that healthy experience, if you're vulnerable and don't have that sense that you can cope and rise beyond the moment, then you fail – and that's what is happening to many of our children today.'

Her professional understanding of the power of children's early experiences was coupled with a very personal commitment to make a positive difference. 'When I was eighteen or nineteen, somebody whom I respected said to me, "Beni, if you don't do something useful with your life, you've wasted it."'

The organisation developed from a small project in a single school. Encouraged by friends, Benita set up her own charity in 1994, and The Place2Be is now working with 37,000 children in 112 schools across England and Scotland, offering children a chance to talk in confidence with an adult. The formula is simple: 'If you have something on your mind, something's troubling you, or you have some good news that you might want to share but you haven't got an adult who has the time, come and talk to us.' It's a formula that works and is establishing itself in a growing number of schools and local authorities. The Place2Be plans to be working with 60,000 children in 170 schools by 2010.

As Benita explained, one of the key lessons she has learnt is that it takes time to get involved in the life of a school and to build up the trust of teachers and parents. The Place2Be introduces itself into a new school by working with the whole school, through assemblies, staff meetings and talks in class, raising issues of emotional well-being and highlighting the importance of understanding children's behaviour. It then goes on to establish a cluster, or hub, of six to ten schools in a local authority area, with each school having its own project manager. The project manager gets to know the children, the teachers and the parents. 'The most important thing is to gain the confidence of everybody involved in the school system.'

In time, a dedicated Place2Be room is established, equipped with puppets, sand trays, playdough and dolls of different ethnic backgrounds. Initially, adults referred the children who came to the Place2Be rooms, but in 1997, and still only working in a handful of schools, Benita and her team tried an experiment. 'We ran a small pilot, a drop-in service run at lunchtime, to which children could refer themselves. We called it The Place to Talk and now 70 per cent of all the children we work with refer themselves rather than being referred. We introduce The Place to Talk in the second half of the first term. If the children want to talk to someone, they put a little slip in the Place to Talk box, and then the school project manager sees them during their lunchtime. They talk about anything: quarrels with friends, bullying, worries about their home life, bereavement, anxiety around exams or the transfer to secondary school, and of course serious issues like domestic violence or harmful behaviours.

'So that's how we slowly embed ourselves in a school. During the first term we take referrals from the teachers, and when

173

parents begin to trust us, they refer their children as well. We now also have a dedicated parent worker in some of our hubs, and we can refer parents for deeper long-term work. Because they see that we make a difference to their child, parents who have often refused support from anyone else trust us enough to accept counselling support for themselves. I believe The Place2Be works because in each school we become an integral part of the system but at the same time we're known to be a separate organisation. The parents perceive the school differently because they see the school is providing something for their children and for them. So the relationships all round begin to grow and develop.'

Benita's ambitious plans to expand and enhance the work of The Place2Be are informed and inspired by the results of their extensive evaluations, on which the organisation puts strong emphasis. 'We built annual reviews into our reporting strategy, and so we go along and we hear directly from the schools about the impact we're having. And that is the most stimulating thing, because we are making a difference. We hear the most extraordinary stories of the difficulties and challenges that children and their families face, and that teachers face. And we also hear of the results that our work has had. We evaluate everything we do, so we've got the data that shows us that we're making a difference. And that really is the motivating factor: knowing that you're making a difference and knowing that you can evidence it and hear it, and hear from the parents about the changes in their children.'

While the strength of Benita's passion and personality are clearly vital factors in her organisation's success, she was keen to explain how much she has learnt about the power of working together as a team. 'One of the major lessons has been that no one person is central to an organisation. From day one we've had fantastic trustees, we've had professional advisers, and I realised that I am able to say, "I don't have the answer", and I can ask other people what the answer is. The school project managers, the volunteers who do the direct work, and the hub managers always humble me. There are superbly dedicated people out there: the teachers, head teachers, school governors and those who volunteer their time. They are totally committed to the well-being of the children. There are a huge number of people seriously joined up in what they hope for their children, so it's not just one person. What has fuelled my passion is meeting fantastic people out there who believe in what we do. And if somebody puts their trust in you, that's a motivating factor. It makes you even more determined to deliver. The trust that people put in you is incredibly humbling.'

Many aspects of modern life have increased the pressures upon children, and it is vital that we do everything we can to support parents and teachers in their efforts to ensure all our children grow up happy and loved and equipped to cope with the adult world. Since she began this work in 1994, Benita told me, she believes the problems facing children have become much more serious: problems of depression, the impacts of long-term unemployment, parental drug and alcohol abuse, and the range of pressures facing children. Her work is providing a vital benefit to schools across the country, enabling them to become what they each aspire to be; a safe and nurturing environment in which children can learn and grow and thrive, and in which they are supported in all aspects of their development and well-being.

Benita reflected on her experiences of building The Place2Be into the organisation she leads today. 'I think The Place2Be has given me much more than I've given it. It's taught me a lot more than I've taught it. It's taught me how to run a business. It's taught me what people need from a leader. It's taught me where my weaknesses are. So I think when you become really involved and passionate about something, you get more from it than you put in.' And when I ask her about what she would say to anyone else thinking about following her example, she says, 'I would say follow your heart. Think about what makes a difference for you, what makes you feel an involved and active member of our society, and think about what you care about and where you'd like to make a difference, and you can. You can make a difference in so many ways. It might only be to one single person's life, but we all have that opportunity. You have to have a sense of belief and passion but also realism: you've got to think "I believe passionately" but also "I can achieve something realistically". I think the message that government – or anyone in a leadership role – needs to give is that if you believe, you can do it. Think about the people you need to help you to do what you want to do. And think about what it would feel like if you were in the position of the people that you want to help. You've got to step out of yourself and be genuine, have integrity.'

24

SAM CONNIFF AND MICHELLE CLOTHIER

People are quite used to the idea: 'If I work, I will get something back', but at the same time don't see the counterbalance: 'If I don't give something, then I will lose out.'

M eet Sam Conniff and Michelle Clothier, two dynamic social entrepreneurs based in Brixton, south London, and you can see how they're going to change things. They have set out to see if the power of marketing can be harnessed for positive effect, and they're doing something unique: applying one of the most modern techniques, youth marketing, to one of the most enduring of challenges, helping young people fulfil their potential. The result is their flourishing youth marketing agency, Livity, and their successful youth training initiative, Live. And now they are planning their next endeavour: an enterprise hub housing thirty local businesses, each of whom will commit to doing something for young people.

Sam explained the original thinking that led to Livity. 'We've always had quite a set theory around community and business. We wanted to prove that you can run a successful business and achieve client objectives, whilst at the same time creating an environment that wasn't horribly stressful for the human beings who worked in it: they could actually develop, and it wasn't just a job. Importantly, above your people and above the profit, could you also produce something with a positive benefit to society? Why shouldn't you be able to, especially when you're dealing with something as significant as marketing and communications helping to shape people's lives and self-identities?'

As Michelle explained, their thinking had been informed by their own professional backgrounds in marketing and their experiences of living and working amongst Brixton's youth. 'We both were youth marketers. I was working for a youth marketing agency on fairly big brands, and Sam had already set up his own youth-focused enterprise. We were good at communicating messages and selling stuff to young people but had become slightly jaded and were asking, "How do we use our skills and experience to more positive effect?" That was how the whole Livity story started.'

Sam picked up the story. 'It got to the point where I couldn't live with the fact that I was selling another mobile phone or presenting these trainers as "the thing you must have" and then walking out of my office in Brixton and home to Streatham – the place that I've always lived – and seeing groups of young men that the papers would have us believe we should all be terrified of who want the latest mobile phone or who help to identify themselves with head-to-toe branded sportswear because there's something missing in their lives. Those kids occasionally do terrible things to get their hands on that stuff; it gives them a sense of actualisation, it's an achievement of some description. They're not finding that in other parts of their lives, so they will go to great lengths to get it. Once you've made that realisation, how can you disassociate yourself from the cycle?

'That to me was one of the turning points when I really realised the symbiotic nature of business in the community and that business will never succeed if the community is falling apart around it. What's the point of me making loads of profit running a company only to be jacked in my nice car 200 metres up the road by the same kids I'm trying to convince need the car? Once you've got to that point, you can't really turn back. But then you've got to do something. You only do what you can where you are with what you've got around you. We're not going to change society or anything like that, but what if we could prove that a business could be a fun place to work, that it could be a positive experience to its employees, that you could make money and the work that you did had a measurable, lasting impact?'

And for Michelle, their work has taken on a very personal meaning, too. 'I had a baby about three years ago, and now, as a parent and a business owner and someone who works within the community, I have more of a personal reason to try and make our surroundings that much better. So that's been quite a big turning point for me. I've got a real, real reason to do that now.'

Livity operates as a socially-minded youth marketing agency, working on campaigns and communications that target and engage with a youth audience. The company's remit is to work with both public- and private-sector clients, as Sam explained. 'The idea is that with a youth audience, the public sector will often have a better understanding of the motivators and drivers, because they deal on the more issues-based side of things. Yet the private sector is often better at executing successful communications, because they're more ruthlessly brand focused and don't have to worry so much about the other stuff. If you pull those two things together, we think that's a really interesting place to achieve necessary and important social objectives, but to use a lot of the brand equity and credibility and commercial-minded approach to achieve them. Increasingly, we like to bring the public and private sectors together on a particular issue.'

Alongside Livity, Sam and Michelle now run a social enterprise called Live, a youth training initiative that developed out of one of Livity's projects and that demonstrates their approach to marketing. 'We were briefed by the local authority to communicate tough, slightly boring messages to thirteen

179

to nineteen year olds about important things: local youth provision, healthy eating, sexual health and careers advice. Our strategy is to involve young people meaningfully in the process. The project itself was a piece of communications work and the magazine we produced, *Live*, was a success and became a training vehicle and an entity in its own right. Whilst Livity was also a socially led idea, with Live forming within it, we couldn't just let it come to a close when the project ended. So we took a fairly major decision to follow our ethics through to their natural conclusion, which led to us forming this youth training programme alongside, making a significant dent on our revenue.'

Live is now a highly successful youth magazine, produced entirely by young people from south London under the mentorship of professional journalists, designers and photographers. It forms the basis of a youth training organisation, offering training and work opportunities in media and communications to a wide range of local young people. 'We've got young offenders, multiple young offenders, refugees, single parents, right through to really bright kids that are in their final year doing a degree who are doing extraordinarily well.' Alongside formalised training, one-to-one mentoring relationships are key to *Live*'s success. 'We have mentors from *Time Out*, *Vogue*, the *Evening Standard* and *thelondonpaper*; kids can just drop in and informally be hooked up at their own speed or pace to doing something that interests them. What we like to do is pair them up with one of the huge number of professionals who volunteer, and then it works really well. If you can then pair one of them up with a journalist, especially if they see the journalist in the paper, then you get those one-on-one relationships beginning to happen.'

The two organisations – the marketing agency Livity and the youth training project Live – sit alongside each other, sharing a buzzing office environment and feeding off each other's ideas and talents. Opportunities to work on Livity projects provide valuable real-life training for the young people, while working so closely with these young people gives Livity's marketing a business advantage. When Sam and Michelle described examples of their work, the benefits of this symbiotic relationship became clear.

Livity created a campaign for the Department of Education and Skills' teenage pregnancy unit as part of the Want Respect campaign, which aimed to reach out to disengaged young people who would not be attracted by traditional advertising and marketing methods that the Government might usually use. Michelle explained how Livity was able to meet the brief and deliver a successful campaign. 'Because we surround ourselves with young people every day and every week and every month, we had experienced the popularity of listening to lyrics and commenting on and discussing and debating them. We came up with a campaign Rhyme4Respect: a nationwide lyric-writing competition based around the subject of respect for yourself and respect for others when it comes to sexual relationships. The competition involved writing lyrics for one of your musical heroes to record. We hooked up with radio and TV stations and retailers, and we brought brands in to give it credibility and relevance and distribution. The theme of the campaign had come to us because we surround ourselves with young people, but then our experience of working with brands was really the thing that allowed us to implement something that reached people in a credible and relevant way.' Recent evaluations have shown that Rhyme4Respect achieved high levels of recognition amongst its target audience and is beginning to have impressive results.

Running the youth training programme alongside a commercial marketing agency allows Sam and Michelle to engage young people in a genuine business approach, and they stressed how central this emphasis is to their success. 'Whether you're talking about Livity or Live, we're running a business here. Anyone participating is coming to join a business and we truly believe that that approach is why young people very quickly engage with what's on offer here. For some young people, for whatever reason, the education system isn't working, they might not be in any employment or any training, and they don't know what their options are. I think we create something here which is a safe place in a way, but it's also very inspiring and it's a place that is full of opportunity.'

What is most striking about Sam and Michelle is the ease with which they combine business acumen and drive with care and empathy for each of the young people whose lives they touch. They have created a dynamic business and a safe and welcoming place that engages with young people on their own terms and gives them opportunities to develop their talents and ambitions. The stories they recount offer a moving insight into the impact they have been able to make on the lives of young people in the area.

Michelle told me, 'We have had kids who have come out of Feltham [the Young Offender Institution and Remand Centre]. This is the first place they come at 7.15 in the morning when they arrive off the train. When you turn up, they're sitting on the doorstep, and the last time it happened, the kid said, "I just need to do something." That's so often the case: they just need a sense of purpose to their day before they go and do what they used to do. As the years go by, we kind of get better at sensing it. They say, "I want to get back involved with the magazine", and we say, "Well, OK, come back any time", and they just stand looking at you at 7.15 in the morning, so we say, "OK, do you want to be kept busy today?" We'll put people to work quite readily, quite easily.'

Sam added his own memories of individuals whose stories have stayed with them and who continue to inspire their work. 'We managed to get one boy onto the Jamie Oliver *Fifteen* programme as one of the apprentice chefs. He got through the 300 to be there in the last fifteen. He's come back to see us about three times, and each time he's just a changed person, not the slightly off-key worrying kid. He's turned into more and more of a confident, successful young man who knows that he has changed his own fortunes – when he was ready. It's nice to know that we provide a constant place that's there for people for when they are ready. From where he started, he's made bigger leaps and bounds than we ever have in a shorter amount of time – yes, with a bit of a boot from us, but he's grabbed the chance and he's going to make something of himself, and I think, "If you can, I can do more."'

Sam and Michelle have built an innovative and important example of how a successful business model can benefit young people. But far from being satisfied with what they have achieved so far, their boundless energy and creativity fills them with ideas of new projects and new possibilities to pursue. 'The ultimate irony of the universe,' said Sam, 'is that individuals are sitting going, "Oh, I can't make any difference, what's my little thing going to do?" and yet the weird thing is, that's what everyone says. It doesn't seem to me like it's that much rocket science to address some of the major issues that we're facing. You've got thousands of young people not in education or employment or training, and these are the ones most at risk of getting into crime, one of the base points which further destabilise society and then have an effect on the economy and everything around it. What if you got thousands of firms of more than 100 people to change their graduate placement for a year and take some lad out of Brixton, just drop him in there and watch the response. An alarm clock and a nine-to-five job will change those boys' lives and knock the naughtiness out of them, and they will be taken seriously after two weeks when everyone realises that they're all right. I would argue that you would have a minimum 50 per cent success rate of changing those people's lives. Doesn't seem that illogical or difficult to me.'

And these aren't just ideas but plans that the Livity team are trying to turn into reality in their local area. Their next plan is to develop a major office space in the area to serve as a hub of social enterprise. The hub would house up to thirty small businesses, along with a media centre and cooking facilities for use in training, with each business receiving subsidised rent in return for hosting a young person at risk as an apprentice. Live would sit at the heart of the project and help to support the young people, who would use the space to engage in training and work opportunities. Sam and Michelle have very big ambitions for how their model could spread, and hearing them explain not only the values but the logic that underpins their work, one can't help but feel that they may just have what it takes to realise their dreams.

'There are things that everyone can do. We do all have responsibility and we are all part of this, and we are all responsible to one another and to our society. The rewards are there for you. People are quite used to the idea: "If I work, I will get something back", but at the same time don't see the counterbalance: "If I don't give something, then I will lose out", and that's a very odd ideology for society to have, I think.'

25

ANTHEA HARE

Being able to provide appropriate care and support at the end of a child's life is the essential point of the work we do.

To witness young children suffering and fighting a losing battle for life is the worst experience in anyone's life. But Anthea Hare has found a remarkable way of helping children and parents at their moments of agony. A pioneer in her field, Anthea is the founder and life president of the Richard House Hospice, the first children's hospice in London. It has been her lifetime's work to build Richard House, and for families in east London who have the most acute need for emotional and practical support, it provides amazing help. Hers is a mission inspired by her professional experiences as a paediatric nurse and by her personal experiences of her severely autistic late brother Richard, who died aged twenty-six.

The history of Richard House is the story of a long and at times challenging journey, which began with Anthea's experiences over many years of service in the NHS. 'I trained as a sick-children's nurse in the 1960s at the Children's Hospital in Birmingham. Between 1974 and 1987, I worked at the Royal London Hospital in Whitechapel, where I joined the paediatric team as a ward sister and later became a nurse teacher. Over the years, I became increasingly aware of the needs of children with life-limiting and life-threatening illnesses and their families, which could not be adequately met through the NHS. I firmly believe that I and all my multi-disciplinary colleagues did our best to support the families, but what every child and family needed was somebody to accompany them on their journey, just somebody who had the time to listen to what they were really saying.'

Her experiences as a professional working directly with families over many years meant that Anthea, like many working in the public services, was best placed to understand their needs and to identify how existing provision could be extended to provide for a need that was not already being met. 'All too often we said goodbye to families at the ward door without actually knowing what would happen to them afterwards. Some of those families came back to see us: I remember they brought toys for the playroom and raised money for things like scanners that the hospital needed. And to these brave people, really we were their friends as much as their professional carers. They taught me more than anybody else about the needs of incredibly sick children with life-threatening illnesses, and the needs of their families, which of course encompasses every aspect of their humanity. Much of what I learnt from these families became the foundation stone for Richard House.'

In the early days, Anthea worked largely on her own, determined to realise her vision. But she is insistent that the final achievement of this vision was very much a group effort, and insistent that all those involved receive the recognition they deserve. 'Professionally, I'd seen this need for a very long time, so I felt, you know, let's get on and do it. Over the months and years, of course, I was joined by others, some of whom were personal friends or introduced to me by friends and professional colleagues. All these people brought to the project their unique skills. They believed in my vision and wanted to see it come to fruition, and they gave of their time and energy willingly, attending meetings, helping me to write letters and always offering me support when I felt discouraged.'

Richard House now provides services for 150 families and

can care for up to eight children at any one time, providing one-to-one care for them and their families. As the hospice has developed, it has expanded to provide a range of services to sick children and their families, including respite care, care within the home, family support and bereavement support. But its core function has always been clear to Anthea. 'Being able to provide appropriate care and support at the end of a child's life is the essential point of the work we do. Any hospice is about death and dying, and however good your respite care is – and most of the work at a children's hospice is respite care – if you get it wrong at the end of that child's life, it might as well go out the window. We were always very clear that the child would die wherever was best for the child and the family, and if that was at home then of course we would facilitate that. But if the family couldn't cope or it was more appropriate, then the child would come into the hospice. We always work in the best interest of the child.'

Anthea is very professionally driven, and her experiences as a healthcare professional inform all her work. But equally important in the very difficult mission she set herself were the experiences she had within her own family. As she explained, the hospice is named after her late brother Richard. 'When Richard was born, he was severely autistic, although at that time the word autism was hardly heard of, and, sadly, all children in those days with a learning disability were classified as mentally retarded; special educational needs were inadequately addressed. All too often doctors used to say to parents, "Put your child in a home and get on with your life." My parents and many other parents certainly didn't do that. Richard died suddenly in 1971 from septicaemia and pneumonia; he was twenty-six. Shortly before he died, the diagnosis of severe autism was confirmed by psychiatrists at the long-stay hospital where he spent the second thirteen years of his life. I have no doubts at all that my personal experiences as a sibling influenced my professional practice as a paediatric nurse and, I believe, gave me a greater understanding of the needs of children with profound disabilities and their families.'

Anthea's experiences continue to inform Richard House and its range of innovative services supporting whole families and in particular the attention it pays to the lives of the brothers and sisters of sick children. 'I think one thing that has thrilled me more than any other, possibly because in a way it's personal, is what is known as our befriending service. We give training to volunteers so they are equipped to befriend family members and siblings of sick children. Occasionally it's been a mum, I think occasionally a grandma, but by and large it's been brothers and sisters. If I could have had that support when I was a child and a teenager, it would have made quite a difference to my early life.'

While the primary focus of Richard House is always the interests of the child, the services it offers bring wide-reaching benefits to the families involved and to local health services and professionals. 'Families that previously had limited or no care and support are now receiving it, and the number is growing as more and more families hear about us. Let's think about what our work allows these families to do. By providing respite care, whether it be day care or overnight care or care in the family's home, not only can you improve the integrity and unity of that family and allow them to function more "normally", but you allow them to have time out together, to have the chill-out time to take their other children out to films or to a theme park. You may also be allowing, if there are two parents, one parent to go back into work. It improves the general health of those parents, and it can also allow them to go back into education, improving their self-esteem. So their caring ability also becomes stronger, and ultimately we're saving the Government money, because there are fewer visits to doctors or to counsellors.'

Richard House is continuing to develop and innovate in response to the changing needs of sick children and their families. Thanks to modern medicine and nutritional techniques, many more children and young people are now surviving conditions that were previously terminal and living longer than we would previously have expected, bringing new challenges and opportunities. 'The need just grows and grows, and needs change all the time. In one sense, it's a positive. These children are now becoming young people, and these young people are now surviving. They are probably more disabled, but they are surviving, and so we as a group here are beginning to look at the developing needs: what happens to these young people once they get to eighteen, nineteen, when officially they're not meant to be here? Where do they go? One of the things we're looking at at the moment is the continuing care of young adults.'

I wonder if many of us could find the strength to do what Anthea and her team do, dealing with pain and tragedy every day and yet remaining incredibly focused on the task in hand. For Anthea, there is a job to do and an opportunity to bring vital care and support to families at their most difficult moments. Reflecting on her own journey in setting up Richard House, Anthea had a word of advice for others. 'If I went right back to the beginning, I would ask, "Why do you want to get involved?" My first question would be, either if you're getting a team together or if you want to be involved personally, to be very clear in your mind why you're doing this. You might have been through some terrible experiences and want to do something positive about it, as many people have done, but I'm very clear that I could never have done it on my own.'

There is an extraordinary courage to be found amongst those who support us through the darkest moments of our lives. When I think of those whom I have met – the healthcare workers, the counsellors, the carers – who tend to the sick and the dying and care for the bereaved, I am deeply moved by their selflessness. And I am moved by the strength it must take to spend every day facing things most of us spend a lifetime hoping we never have to deal with, in order to be a comfort to those who desperately need it.

26

SHARON BERRY

The children of prisoners are more likely to become prisoners themselves if we don't stop dads from reoffending. So helping maintain family ties is something that benefits the whole of society.

'Ten years ago I was a barmaid. Last year I had to give a speech at Buckingham Palace and another at the Home Office. I never would have believed I could do stuff like that. It just goes to show what you can do if you've got something to believe in.'

Sharon Berry runs a charity called Storybook Dads, which is transforming the lives of thousands of children around the country and changing the way we deal with those adults we send to prison. 'Its aim is to maintain contact between imprisoned parents and their children during their period of incarceration. And the way we do that is to record the parent reading a story for their child, either one they've read from a book or one they've made up themselves, which we then download onto a computer. We take out the mistakes and put in sound effects and music, and then burn it onto a CD and send it to the child. That's it in a nutshell.'

So, the idea is simple but life changing: instead of prisoners largely out of contact with their children, and children denied the encouragement of their parent, dads send their kids their stories and are supported to help ensure they never lose touch with their family.

The journey that took Sharon to a recording studio in Dartmoor prison started ten years ago when she decided to become the first ever member of her family to go to university and study for a degree. 'I didn't even know anybody who had been to university and it was all a bit scary, but I loved it.' She loved it so much that after graduation she began a Masters degree and started training in radio production at BBC Radio Devon. An appeal came into the radio station asking for help in setting up and running a prison radio station, and Sharon volunteered because she knew how to use the software. 'The writer-in-residence at the prison asked me to take over and develop an offshoot of the radio station – the story-recording scheme – and we used the audio equipment to produce prisoners' stories. It's not a new thing for prisoners to send stories to their children, but it had always been done on a tape recorder. By using digital technology, I realised we could edit and enhance the recording and make something much more professional. So that's what I started doing. I was teaching as well, but gradually I realised how popular the story idea was, and how great the need for it was, so I stopped teaching, set up Storybook Dads as a charity, and it's grown from there.'

With no funding, Sharon started the project on her own. That was just four years ago. Today, Storybook Dads has six staff, although Sharon is the only full-timer, and a substantial team of volunteers, many of whom are prisoners themselves. In her first year she was able to produce just forty-four stories. In 2006, the figure was more than 1,100. In between, she has raised more than half a million pounds and put in more hours than she cares to remember. But what drives her and her colleagues is the knowledge that, with the prison population at 80,000, the need for Storybook Dads grows greater every day. 'This scheme is a lifeline for lots and lots of families, because there are about 150,000 children affected by the imprisonment of a parent each year and about half of all prisoners lose contact with their families while they're in custody. We're trying to give parents a chance to do something tangible for their children and to believe in themselves as good parents. And it's not just their own children. It might be a little brother or sister, or a grandchild or a niece. It's all about family ties. That's the important thing. So, whatever the relationship, if the child is close to them, we let them do a story. What also keeps us going is listening to those children and realising how important it is for them. They haven't committed a crime, but when their parent goes to prison, they feel abandoned and isolated, shamed and unloved. And if there's no intervention, they are likely to be the next generation of offenders.

'So, it works for the parents and it works for the children. The statistics are that something like 25 per cent of prisoners have spent time in care or been brought up in care, as opposed to 2 per cent of the general population. I'm not making excuses for prisoners by any means, but sometimes when you hear about the kind of upbringing they've had, you realise that a lot of them have never been read to as a child or read to their own children. It's like breaking new ground for them, and when they're reading a story for the first time, you can almost see that it's like a child reading for the first time. The reward is just letting them engage with the magic of storytelling with their child. That's what motivates me: just seeing the results and hearing them say what a difference it makes to their child.'

Storybook Dads started in Dartmoor prison and that remains the centre of Sharon's project. She works from an editing suite that at the beginning was simply an empty cell. But there are now thirty-five prisons involved, sending their stories on minidiscs to Dartmoor, where they are edited, and a further fifteen prisons have set up their own editing teams. At Dartmoor, prisoners are trained how to use the audio equipment and can get a qualification in sound and audio production. 'We're sort of rolling it out throughout the prison estate,' says Sharon. 'More and more prisons have become women's prisons, so at some point we'll have to change our name and call it Storybook Dads and Mums, but when I started this I didn't know it was going to become what it has become. I just know we've got to keep rolling it out through the whole of England and Wales. We've helped three schemes set up in Scotland as well, but that's the Scottish prison service, and once we've set them up they're on their own, really. But it just grows and grows and grows. We can't stop it now! At first I would go out and tell prisons about it, but, prison being as it is, news gets around very quickly and now, if ever I'm walking around a prison wing, people will come up to me and say, "Miss, miss, you're Storybook Dads, aren't you? Can I do a story for my kiddie?"'

The project holds a selection of books from which prisoners can read. All the children's classics are popular, as well as some of my own kids' favourites, *The Gruffalo* and *The Snail and the Whale*. There are also writing workshops where prisoners can receive help and advice in creating their own stories, so improving – or acquiring – writing skills as well as reading skills. Sharon explained, 'If the prisoners do write their own story, they can also illustrate it, type it up and create a bound laminated book which is sent out along with the CD so the child can read along as they listen to the story their dad has written for them, which, often as not, features the child as the hero or heroine. If a prisoner can't read, a mentor can read a story line by line for them to repeat, and then the story is edited together afterwards. And if they don't want to read a story, prisoners can record audio letters instead. The next development, already under way, is to introduce DVD Dads, so that parents can be filmed reading at the beginning of their story, perhaps with some simple animation and drawings to illustrate the narrative as it moves along.

'The feedback we get from families is just amazing. They tell us the children love these CDs because it's something that empowers them. It's something they can listen to whenever they're missing their dad. They take it to school to the show-and-tell sessions. They take it in the car to listen to, they listen to it at night, and they take it and play it to their grandparents. They just love their CDs. The production standard is very professional. We edit out all the mistakes and extraneous noises, and we put in sound effects. So, if there are wizards or dragons or animals, we can put all the right sound effects in and create a very polished product. A story that takes ten minutes to read may take three to four hours to edit properly. And all the time the prisoners are begging me for another one, and we have to say, "Well, you've got to wait three months." We can't keep up with demand.'

Sharon's work has helped thousands of families, and the organisation has grown far bigger than she ever imagined. She knows that something as simple as the chance to read a bedtime story to your child, or to be read a story from a parent far away, can be profoundly important for parents and children alike. It can make them feel safe and loved, cared about and remembered. And it can help strengthen the bonds that keep families together during tough times. It is something every parent who is separated from their child should have the chance to do, and, inspired by Sharon's work, the army got in touch. With Sharon's help, they have now set up Storybook Soldiers for men and women serving in Iraq and Afghanistan.

The outcomes of Storybook Dads can be very far-reaching, because as well as the emotional benefits for prisoners and their children, as well as strengthening family bonds and as well as improving prisoners' skills, Sharon is keen to stress the longer-term impact this type of work can have. 'The Home Office states that maintaining family ties significantly helps to reduce reoffending, and this is well documented. There's got to be more effort put into it. There's hardly any statutory funding for prisoners' families, it's nearly all charitable stuff. Just throwing more and more people in prison, getting tougher and tougher on crime, all that does is take someone away from his family, put him in prison, he loses his job, his family might break down, and then he's never going to get back on the straight and narrow, is he? There needs to be more funding directed at it. The children of prisoners are more likely to become prisoners themselves if we don't stop dads from reoffending. So helping maintain family ties is something that benefits the whole of society. When it costs something like £35,000 a year to keep a man in jail, plus another £35,000 for his court costs, it would be money well spent if we could invest more in trying to maintain family ties and stop the children developing mental-health problems and ending up in care themselves, making this an endless cycle.'

Sharon never set out to work with prisoners, and her journey from barmaid to teacher to Storybook Dads was an unexpected one, so what motivates her to devote her life to this work? 'It's the prisoners. It's talking to them and working with them. People can be very judgmental about prisoners, and I guess I used to be. I had no idea what to expect the first time I went into a prison. But, of course, once you get in there you realise that they are just normal young men, but most of them have taken a wrong path. I'm not making any excuses for them, but with the right input we can turn things round and stop the reoffending, which is crippling in a country where the jails are already bulging.'

What does she think are the lessons that she's learnt from these whirlwind years? 'I think tenacity and just keeping at it, because it can be difficult to get things going in prison. It really can be hard. Although there's a lot of people who believe in what we're doing, sometimes the red tape and the security can be just so off-putting. Governors can change. Policies change. Premises are always incredibly difficult to find. And just pulling a project together and satisfying the security department and stuff like that can be a bit like wading through treacle. But we've managed to do it, and we've come a long way. The high point is the feedback that we get from the families and the prisoners. The prisoners often say it's the best thing they've ever done since they've been in jail. They find it really rewarding and have a great sense of achievement.'

27

TOM SAVAGE

I'm focused on trying to fly the flag for social
enterprise and make sure that young people are
not just thinking about making money but also
about changing people's lives.

The day I talked to Tom Savage he'd just started another
new company. I planned to talk to him about his success
in founding Blue Ventures, a marine conservation and travel
company, and his commitment to promoting social enterprise
among young people. And I wanted to congratulate him on
being named Young Social Entrepreneur of the Year at the
age of twenty-six. But as I talked to him about Blue Ventures,
he was already talking about his latest venture: Bright Green
Talent, a new recruitment agency specialising in jobs for
people in the environmental and corporate social responsibility
movements.

What makes Tom tick and gives him his boundless energy
and creativity is both his love for business and his deeply held
belief that business can be a force for social good. And this
started very young. His entrepreneurial curiosity began with
the family business. 'My dad bought the company he owns for
£1 and built it up into a successful company. I don't think he's
necessarily an entrepreneur, but he demonstrated to me the
lifestyle of somebody who is in control of their own destiny
and can run with their own ideas.

'I've always been very interested in business. When I was

young and people asked me what I wanted to do, I always said, "I want to do everything", and entrepreneurship gives you the chance to do a lot of stuff in your day-to-day work. One day you'll be doing marketing, the next day you'll be doing some legal stuff, the next day you'll be accounting and the next you'll be trying to sell stuff.'

With business in the genes, Tom's two business degrees and a brief stint in the City could have led to great commercial success. So what was it that persuaded him to apply his business aptitude not to the pursuit of profit but to a different end altogether? 'There is a quote which gives the flavour of it from Adam Smith in 1776. He says, "No society can surely be flourishing and happy, of which the far greater part of the members are poor and miserable." Which I think is a truism. How can we say that we are a "developed nation" if the majority of the world's population haven't got access to x, y and z?'

Tom's interest in enterprise developed whilst studying at Edinburgh University, where he founded the Entrepreneurial Society. 'There were 15,000 people at Edinburgh, we all had great ideas, then we went to the pub and forgot about them. So I started this organisation, which was essentially trying to get people together to talk about doing something together.'

After graduating, Tom founded his first company, Blue Ventures, when he and another university friend started running diving expeditions to Madagascar and Tanzania. 'I said, "Look, why are we going out there and spending six weeks setting up an operation only to come home again? There's no sustainability in that. Why don't we, instead of raising the money, get the place started and then have other people raise money to come and visit?"

'Blue Ventures is focused on marine conservation. It's a social company, a normal company with a charitable arm, and all the profits of the company get donated across the charity. The focus of the work is to use that model of social enterprise to do conservation work in parts of the western Indian Ocean where it is desperately needed. At the moment we work in south-west Madagascar. We take about 100 to 120 volunteers away a year, and we charge them for their expedition of six weeks. They go on a trip, and we teach them how to dive, teach them all about the science we're doing there and involve them in a number of initiatives with the community. So we invest money, employ local staff and bring in the additional resource of volunteers' time, as well as spearheading a research initiative.'

Blue Ventures is now a successful award-winning business but one which Tom and his co-founder have not taken any profit from. Deciding to run Blue Ventures on a non-profit basis was not a difficult decision for Tom; it just made sense, both morally and from a business point of view. 'I always felt that business could do a lot more than go out and sell, sell, sell and do everything you can to make a profit, even if it's at the expense of the next person. There are lots of organisations making very healthy profits, which are also giving something back. We went a bit more extreme than that because we didn't feel that the conservation work that we were doing fitted with profit. We felt that if we were making any surplus on the back of what we were doing, then we had to plough that back into the local community. We wanted to take away that potential for greed, we wanted to make sure that our outlook and our workload was focused on conservation and not on lining our pockets. And the second issue is that we also felt that the people who were coming to work on the projects would be less inclined to work as hard or to be as committed if we were just a profit-making organisation. So there were kind of two pulls and pushes. We felt that we really could make enough to live and make a significant difference. We went an unusual route. Most people would probably go and make a boatload of money and then go and start a foundation or a charity or something. Whereas we had to kind of beg, steal and borrow to get the ventures off the ground.'

Tom continues to develop a range of other social enterprises, which focus on enabling people to find simple ways to make a difference to the planet. These include a socially responsible travel company. 'My feeling is that travelling responsibly is a no-brainer in that it's not any more expensive and you get a much better holiday. If you stay in a locally run place, then the people know about your area, they care more about you, and they care more about the local area as well. I started something else quite recently called TipThePlanet. It is a website – an online Wiki – that encourages people to post tips that are beneficial to the planet. I got pretty fed up with reading in one magazine you should fly, and then in *The Guardian* you shouldn't fly, and then somebody else saying just take short-haul flights and don't go on long-haul flights. And my flatmates were arguing over whether it was better to have an electric or a gas kettle. People are always saying you should recycle, and I thought nobody really knows the right answer. The nature of our website is that anybody can add to it, anybody can edit it.'

Tom's passion for social enterprise means he is not content to run his own businesses but is now a leading campaigner working to get young people involved in thinking about enterprise for social benefit. He has been working for the Make Your Mark campaign aimed at inspiring young people to use enterprising ideas for social or environmental change. Among the range of initiatives he has helped to develop there was the amazing Make Your Mark with a Tenner campaign in which 1,000 young people across the UK were loaned £10 each and challenged to see who could make the biggest impact with it in one month, with prizes awarded both for profits and for social impact.

'I'm focused on trying to fly the flag for social enterprise and make sure that young people are not just thinking about making money but also about changing people's lives. I sit on the Board of Young Enterprise London, and Young Enterprise is an example of learning through doing. If you can give young people a chance to actually go out and get involved – even if they hear a talk, it gets filed away in their minds and five years later they think about it again – we're beginning to initiate change within their processes. Giving people the confidence to think that it's a viable option is really important.'

Tom is convinced that the time is right to encourage young people to engage with a greener, more socially conscious entrepreneurial culture. 'I've been very lucky that the campaign that I'm working with is meeting a rising tide. I think young people are increasingly aspiring to make a difference and make their mark but also to change people's lives. There is significant research that indicates young people are very interested in money, but they are also very interested in making a positive difference.' And this has inspired his latest venture: Bright Green Talent, which Tom was eager to tell me all about. 'I think bright people will be the key to making that movement succeed. If I wasn't going to go and start another business, then what I would really like to do is to focus more on the good business campaign. Try to encourage more people to think about how their businesses can be more socially and environmentally minded. More and more young people want to work for a company that does that, whatever role they're in. If you want to attract the brightest talent nowadays, the MBA students, times are changing, and more and more people want to do this work.'

With his passion for ideas, his infectious enthusiasm, and his resolute belief that business can work differently, Tom gives an inspiring insight into what the next generation of business leaders could look like. If, like him, they too refuse to take the easy option; if, like him, they innovate to combine entrepreneurial drive with moral responsibility, then our future will indeed look bright. Or, as Tom himself put it, 'Perhaps one day a millionaire will not just be someone who has made a million pounds but also someone who has changed a million lives.'

28

STEVIE SIEGERSON

*We believe that the young people we're working with
have the answers. We are not here to stuff anything in;
we are here to draw out what's in there already.*

'I left school at an early age. I stopped attending, there were lots of reasons,' Stevie Siegerson recalls. 'My mum was a single parent who looked after seven of us. One thing I do know that helped me change my life was individuals. I can name five different individuals in my life who, by meeting them, and how they helped me, enabled me to make changes and turn my life around. That's what got me here, really.

'When I was about twelve, a youth worker really surprised me by how he reacted when I got into some trouble: he was kind to me. That had such a big, big influence on me. My mum was busy with the rest of the kids; I was just kind of getting caught up in things. At that early stage, meeting this one person just allowed me to make a shift in direction. That started my journey into youth work. I went back to school in my early twenties and did a couple of Highers. I then went to college and got a hunger for learning which has continued throughout my life.'

And it is these changes that he made in his own life that today enable Stevie to help others change their lives. He is part of a remarkable project that is rooted in a belief that people have it in them to be the best that they can be. A few years ago, when Stevie was working with young people in Glasgow, running personal development programmes, he was invited to get together a group of young people and test out the brand-new Columba 1400 centre on the Isle of Skye. The Columba 1400 programmes are based on the belief that those who have weathered tough times have tremendous leadership potential. By tapping into that potential, Columba 1400 encourages individuals to realise their full abilities for their own benefit and for that of the wider community.

Today, Stevie is centre leader at the Columba 1400 Community and International Leadership Centre in Staffin, at the north end of Skye. 'We're not at the end of the world,' he says, 'but we're about a mile away. I can see the end of the world from my window.' He works primarily with young people from 'tough realities', young people whose early lives have been lived in challenging personal and social circumstances. Central to the Columba 1400 philosophy is one of my favourite quotes, repeated in their materials, from the novelist John Buchan: 'Our task is not to put the greatness back into humanity, but to elicit it, for the greatness is there already.'

This strikes a chord with me and so many other people. Stevie explained what makes the Columba 1400 approach unique. 'Our methodology is very simple. We make the assumption that people have in them what they need, and the conditions that we set up as we work with folk elicit that. The core of our task is to bring out what's there already: it's something that resonates throughout everything we do.'

When I heard about his work and his life, I realised that Stevie represented so much that I wanted to express about the power that one-to-one relationships have to transform lives, and the way in which a personal relationship with someone we trust can challenge us to become more than we are. His story is a powerful demonstration of the difference we can make simply by believing in someone. All it took for Stevie to change was for someone to believe that there was more in him than he himself was able to see, and this gave him the strength to bring out the best within himself. Now Stevie devotes his life to being that someone for hundreds of young people each year.

Stevie's life has had its share of difficulties, and with down-to-earth honesty and self-awareness he explained how he came to make the choices that shaped his life. 'Most of the areas where I lived in my early years would be identical to the areas that the young people I work with live in. The son of a single parent myself, I see myself in lots of these kids, and in many ways it allows me to connect with them. I often say, "If I'd had these opportunities, what might have been different for me?"'

Columba 1400 runs residential programmes for young people, as well as for teachers, business leaders and care workers. All of the Columba 1400 programmes are based around six key principles – awareness, focus, creativity, integrity, perseverance and service – themes that are explored in depth during the residential programmes in the inspiring landscape of Skye. By spending time in an environment away from the 'tough realities' of home, participants can experience things and share ideas beyond their everyday lives. 'When participants arrive at the centre, we deliberately try and slow them down so that they can reflect on the different location and the different people they are with. We're in an amazing place, and as they walk up the hill, they'll stop and take in the world and have a wee chat. They will have identified a number of core values that they want to talk about, and they'll write them on wee stones and put them in their pocket. They'll be with a trusted companion and have the space to walk, reflect and challenge themselves.'

I wanted to celebrate the work of Stevie and Columba 1400 because it is one of a number of projects now challenging young people to become better than they are, projects that are realising leadership potential amongst those who might struggle to see it within themselves, such as Changemakers, Youth Action Network, Youth at Risk, Common Purpose and Weston Spirit.

I am fascinated by their week-long programmes that gradually bring out the best in young people. The Columba 1400 team start by asking participants to reflect on the core values that shape our lives, and then they ask people what they really value. Julia Ogilvy, the founder of Project Scotland, which is getting hundreds of young people into community action through volunteering, described to me how she was inspired by a week with some of the young teenagers from one of the most deprived estates in Edinburgh, Wester Hailes. 'We had a chance to be still for a while and to learn the importance of real teamwork. For many, this was the first time they had spoken to each other outside their own small groups, and many commented that this taught them to be less judgemental, that meeting new people helped their confidence and that they learnt to show more respect and to stay true to themselves. When they talked about what they valued within the community, it was a teacher or charity worker who went the extra mile that was respected. The group wished they were able to speak out and help create change, and that people would really listen to what they had to say. As the week progressed, I saw ambitions change as they began to think of what was possible, in spite of a world in which prospects are incredibly limited and life is often a series of daily battles.'

Columba 1400's programmes have been enormously successful however you try to measure it. 'When anyone comes through our doors, the individual success rates are very high. A recent evaluation showed that of the young folk we were working with who'd been in care, or that horrible phrase "the NEETs" [those not in education, employment or training], around 75 per cent of these young folk were moving on and getting into employment and training.

'Some of the outcomes are easier to identify, but, as most people who are working at grass-roots level on this stuff know, some of the most inspirational stories are the ones that might look small but actually have tremendous impact. A couple of weeks ago, we had two sisters who just could not stand the sight of each other. The whole week, all they did was argue with each other. At the end of the week, we've got a photograph of them graduating: these two young girls hugging each other with tears rolling down their face. Stories like that go a long, long way. All of a sudden, people are appreciating each other a wee bit more, and that will have an effect back in their community.

'We often talk about this idea of the ripple effect: smaller stories that will have such a big, big impact. I have no doubt in my mind that lives have been changed, and some lives are being saved, if I'm honest. It's simple: if you come to a place and you find your fit in the world – in the sense that you find a role and help make a change for other folk – the effect is massive. If it is a head teacher working with their staff, for example, that ripples onto the children in the school and then has an impact in the houses that these guys go home to. None of this is separate, you cannot separate it. The irony is that we talk about this stuff as soft outcomes, whilst it is actually much harder to achieve.'

It is testimony to the impact the centre has had on so many lives that, like Stevie, many other staff members are also graduates of Columba 1400 programmes. 'I think the thing that I'm most proud of here is the people: they just blow me away. One example is a young woman who came here when she was seventeen from a care facility. She inspires people week to week, day to day, whether that's a group of head teachers or a group of chief executives. Sometimes I feel very humbled. My title is Centre Leader, but I get my inspiration from the staff.'

Stevie and his team have hundreds of stories to tell of individual lives transformed. The changes they are able to help bring about in young people from the most challenging of backgrounds are remarkable, and I wondered what it was about Columba 1400 that meant it could succeed where so many others working with these young people had not. 'The vision and mission that Columba 1400 has is much like the vision that lots of other organisations have, but there's something very specific about the idea of young people going through tough realities. We believe that the young people we're working with have the answers. We are not here to stuff anything in; we are here to draw out what's in there already.'

Columba 1400 – and Stevie – don't have a magic formula for success. Their success lies in seeing young people not as the collection of problems with which they have been labelled but as individuals with unique abilities and unique potential. And what is clear above all is that Columba 1400's success lies in the very personal love and care of Stevie and his team, for whom this is very much more than a job. 'Life creates opportunities and possibilities in whatever you do. This work, rather than being something I do, it's something I am.'

29

VIC ECCLESTONE

There are crazy, entrepreneurial people out there in the community . . . who actually make the most profound changes to young people's lives . . . They do it their way; they won't conform. I don't know how one builds policy around people like that, but I think they are the small social entrepreneurs we really need to invest in.

Vic Ecclestone says he has always been intrigued by people saying, 'You can't do that.' After twenty-five years as a teacher in a big comprehensive school set in the middle of south Bristol's huge and sprawling Hartcliffe housing estate, it still intrigues him. 'People say it about children all the time: "They can't do this; they won't do that." It makes me want to say, "So where's the evidence?" Of course, they're not really talking about children. They're talking about their perception of children. We allow ourselves to have such terribly low expectations of kids, especially white working-class teenage boys. There's a lack of expectation about their whole performance, not just their academic performance. It's patronising. When it comes to music, for example, there's an assumption that if you're going to do music on the Hartcliffe estate, it has to be DJ workshops because it's a working-class area. I'm telling you, Hartcliffe is in danger of having more DJs than Ibiza.'

Vic has challenged both the perception and the reality of low expectations. As a special-needs teacher, he ran after-school activities, including camps, visits to the local theatre, sailing trips and climbing trips. Many of the participants had never been out of Bristol, some of them had hardly been off the estate and had never had responsibility for looking after themselves or their possessions. Outwardly tough and worldly wise, they were unable to cook, wash their clothes or look after themselves. 'For me,' explained Vic, 'special education – well, any education – was about extending their experience and giving them choices.'

When a group of fourteen-year-old boys told him they wanted to play cricket, friends and colleagues were sceptical. 'The view was that Hartcliffe kids wouldn't turn up for games, let alone practice. They wouldn't have kit, and if they did, they would forget to bring it.' Vic found someone to coach the boys and a local sports shop owner let them have kit at cost price. 'I was of the opinion that if we were going to play cricket, we were going to do it properly: dress the part and come out looking smart. At our first match, we were all out for thirty-nine, not a great start, I admit, but we had a proper tea afterwards.' His initial group of twenty-two grew rapidly to almost a hundred – young women as well as young men. Soon after that, sponsorship was raised to employ an ex-Somerset county coach whose passion and ability fired up the players. Over the next two years, the cricket expanded to embrace football and weightlifting, and eventually the sports council provided a part-time coordinator to run the whole project.

Vic then decided to turn his attention to the arts. He was sure that if the young people he worked with 'couldn't do' cricket, they certainly 'wouldn't do' opera. He invited Welsh National Opera to the school to perform *Macbeth* in front of 200 spellbound eleven year olds. He contacted the Rambert Dance Company and asked them whether they would be prepared to do some workshops with the school's PE department. At first, only girls wanted to participate, but soon there was a group of boys hanging around the gym door asking, 'Why can't we do this?' Vic persuaded the education department of Birmingham

Royal Ballet to run a series of classes for the boys, culminating in an extraordinary dance performance at the school. 'The Birmingham Royal Ballet did pieces from *Sylvia*. They were so close to the audience you could see the real physicality and strength of the dancers. And then the boys did their piece. The place was packed out – standing ovation.'

This was followed by a regular after-school club for forty boys who began to create a dance piece about the death of the singer Kurt Cobain. Vic explained, 'For them, that was the equivalent to the death of John Lennon and its effect on me. They had a whole series of discussions and lectures with professionals about some of the key things in Cobain's life – alcohol, drugs, family disruption, violence – and they built all that in to the piece with the choreographer and we made a film of it, which we shot in a derelict railway station. For me, the idea really was to put together a wide range of experiences for the boys and then to build on their interest – if they were interested – but allow them to make the choices. I had to have faith in their choices.'

As Vic told me his story, I was struck by a particular trait I have seen in many of the people that have inspired this book. He was driven not by a dramatic personal experience or a self-conscious ethic or mission. There was no magic turning point, no moment of revelation guiding his way. He simply believed things could be better than they were and set about making them so. Vic didn't set out to transform his students or to make radical changes to their lives. He simply believed they could achieve, and aspire to, and become, more than everyone else was telling them they could become. And this belief was all he needed. He took risks, he tried things that many thought impossible, he faced constraints and disappointments, but he kept on going, making things a little better one step at a time.

'As a student, I lived in Manchester with the Twisted Wheel and Northern Soul, so I've never really subscribed to the view that boys don't dance. But I have to admit, when I went to the head teacher and said, "Hey, Tony, I've got forty guys who want to dance with the Birmingham Royal Ballet", he did sort of look at me as though I'd been on the sherry rather early in the day. And the added frisson was that there had been disturbances in Hartcliffe, with shops burnt and so forth, only a month or so earlier.'

As Vic explained, what was so vital to the project's success was that it was not simply an exercise in personal development or artistic exploration but a serious attempt to train the boys to be high-quality dancers. Only through genuine hard work did the boys learn the confidence, discipline and perseverance that was to be the project's legacy. 'When the Birmingham Royal Ballet did dance classes, it wasn't pretend. It wasn't patronising. It was hard. I went in after a class, and there was a young man on the floor with a towel over his head and a bottle of water in his hand, and I said to him, "Are you OK?" and he said, "Yes, but I thought dancers were poofs." So I asked him, "Have you changed your mind?" – not expecting a great philosophical interchange – and he said, "Yes. I've only been doing this for forty minutes, and I'm bloody knackered." What I learnt from the dance company was that the young people quickly saw through patronising and superficial attitudes. I don't think they would have had any respect for a choreographer who pretended that they were doing all right when they weren't. So the relationships they had with the dancers and teachers were real, positive relationships.'

Throughout the project's development, Vic was convinced that, regardless of the challenges of bringing dance to Hartcliffe, it would give his boys a lasting and first-hand understanding of some vital life lessons. 'The serious point those boys learnt from working with the Birmingham Royal Ballet was that when somebody makes something look easy, whether it's a piece of mathematics or a bit of engineering, no matter what it is, you can bet somebody's had to work for twelve or fourteen years to make it look easy. It doesn't happen in an instant.

They learnt that improvement comes through hard work and listening and dedication over a period of time. It's very trendy to talk about transferable skills, but that was exactly what those young people learnt and were able to take into their school life. It's not just me saying that. It's documented by research. One young man told the researchers: "It gave me the confidence to put my hand up in class and say, 'I'm sorry but I don't understand that.'"

Before long, the Hartcliffe Boys Dance Company was working with some 200 boys and putting on performances, first in local theatres, then on London's South Bank and finally doing European tours. 'Dance became quite a normal part of school and lots of dance organisations would phone up and offer to come and teach classes. That flowed over into the feeder junior schools. We ended up teaching 300 children to tap dance on a regular basis – after supplying them with tap shoes – and one of those little kids is now tap dancing professionally.'

Twelve years after that first visit by the Rambert Dance Company, the University of the West of England commissioned research into the impact of the programme. More than a hundred ex-pupils of Hartcliffe school were interviewed. The report found that: 'Dance flourished because it was not an alien culture imposed from above, but because the boys were encouraged and facilitated to find their own ways of expressing themselves.' And as Vic cites with pride, 'Each of the young men interviewed has been in gainful employment, when the circumstances of their boyhood and youth could well have led to different outcomes. That is a positive thing. Each of the young men interviewed has been articulate about empowerment, choice, strength of character, self-esteem and their role as citizens. That is a remarkable thing.'

Looking back over what the project achieved, Vic spoke not only of the lasting effect it had on his students but also of how it continues to challenge the way the estate perceives itself. The purpose of Hartcliffe Boys Dance Company was not to train professional dancers. As Vic says, 'The guys who really got something out of it aren't dancers. They're plumbers and bricklayers. They're working in television. But all of them can articulate that what they had is what they want for their children and for their young people. That makes a difference. Your view could be that the Hartcliffe is a bad estate. Yes, there are bad people. There are bad families. But there's a hidden agenda in highlighting that: "We are worse than somewhere else so give us the money." Does that mean the worse you are, the more money you get? Why don't we sometimes focus on the successful people? We've had leading environmental lawyers and people running successful businesses come out of this estate. An interesting piece of research published in May 2007 suggests that there are between 600 and 800 people living on the estate who have degrees. Where does that appear in the discussion about what kind of a place Hartcliffe is?'

Vic is clear about how much he has learnt from the process and how these lessons could help inform other work with young people. 'I've learnt a number of things from the experience. The first is: it's not a quick fix. Things don't happen in the space of a year or eighteen months. I know it's a cliché, but we really do need to think about long-term investment in young people. The second thing is there are crazy, entrepreneurial people out there in the community who, in my experience, are the people who actually make the most profound changes to young people's lives. It doesn't matter whether they're running a cricket club or a football club, they do it their way; they won't conform. I don't know how one builds policy around people like that, but I think they are the small social entrepreneurs we really need to invest in. And the third thing is we need to look at the fact that a small amount of money for a tiny organisation, say a football club on a housing estate, can have a profound effect on large numbers of young people. It's often not about the tens of thousands or hundreds of thousands of pounds. It's about a few hundred quid.'

Vic's work stands as an example to all those searching for new ways to bring out the best within young people. In his modest and reflective way, Vic makes it sound simple, but his successes are testimony to the inspiring power of those who believe that young people will always rise to meet the challenges we offer them. 'At the end of the day, it's a belief in the power of education, a belief in the power of choice for young people and a belief that, unlike the present fashion for demonising children, giving them the opportunities to take on responsibility is something they want and something they respond to.'

Twelve years on from the start of the dance company, Hartcliffe school has become a specialist business and engineering college. The dance company is a fading legend, but the dancers are not. While having her boiler serviced, a professional dancer living in Bristol was asked by the service engineer what she did for a living. 'I'm a dancer,' she replied. The repairman stuck his head out from behind the boiler. 'That's interesting,' he said. 'I learnt to dance at Hartcliffe.'

30

TOMMY MacKAY

People everywhere were seeking only to do the ordinary and the possible and the things that have been done before. What I was interested in was to ask, 'What could we do that involves tackling the extraordinary and the impossible?'

Ten years ago, Dr Tommy MacKay, a child psychologist from Cardross in Dunbartonshire, had a bold and daring idea: what if it were possible to achieve what no other deprived area anywhere has achieved; what if we could eradicate illiteracy from this area for ever? Tommy MacKay had an ambition, and he put himself and his reputation on the line in order to achieve the impossible.

Today, the West Dunbartonshire Literacy Initiative, which Tommy created, is a landmark scheme that is every day realising his dream. From 20 per cent functional illiteracy amongst school leavers ten years ago, it has now achieved a rate of virtually 0 per cent, and as Tommy presented his findings to me I was convinced that every area of the country could see a similar improvement.

At the root of this extraordinary success has been Tommy's absolute refusal to accept that anything was impossible, a belief nurtured since his childhood. 'Essentially I grew up in poverty in early childhood. It was often the case that we weren't terribly sure where the next meal was coming from. I had the honour of having been born in the one district in Britain that

217

in a national socio-economic survey managed to come lowest in the whole UK for educational outcomes and second lowest in the UK for health outcomes: that's Maryhill in Glasgow. I was born in what we call a single end: one room for our family of four – my mother, father and sister and myself. My father was very ill for all of my early childhood and died when I was three, and my mother was also in very poor health. Things were difficult, and my mother, like many Scots, was too proud to take anything "from the parish". We had very little money. I know that sometimes my sister and I would be sent for errands to the corner shop to ask for a bone for the dog, but they knew perfectly well we didn't have a dog. I must say I came through that environment quite unaware of any exigencies and enjoying the whole thing, because it was marked by extremely positive and upbeat attitudes.'

Tommy's early experiences established a lifelong alignment with the poor and the disadvantaged, and it was his mother's unfailing optimism in particular which has shaped his attitudes to what is possible. 'My mother was a really extraordinary person. She was a shining example of why we should always aim for the impossible and the extraordinary. She was perfectly confident that I would go through the educational system and go to university and be able to do whatever I liked in life. It was a very positive atmosphere.'

Tommy did just that and began a distinguished career as a child psychologist. Throughout his career, his work has always focused on tackling disadvantage. 'I've been used all my life to trekking around some of the darkest alleys at the dead of night, chasing up children and their families. That has very much been a way of life.'

This commitment to tackling deprivation, its causes and effects, took a new direction, when, ten years ago, Tommy began to develop his ambitious plan. 'Ten years ago or just over that, I sent to the director of education in West Dunbartonshire the kind of paper that I imagine most directors of education would think quite interesting and then put into the nearest bin. The paper was entitled "A Vision for Transforming the Reading Achievement of All Children". I was proposing that people everywhere were seeking only to do the ordinary and the possible and the things that have been done before. What I was interested in was to ask, "What could we do that involves tackling the extraordinary and the impossible?" – doing things that have never been done in the world before. The idea was not only to raise reading achievement for everyone but it was to eradicate illiteracy, something that had never been done in the world before anywhere, most especially in areas of socio-economic disadvantage.'

West Dunbartonshire is one of the poorest areas in Britain and the second most economically disadvantaged council area in Scotland. Ten years ago, large proportions of its children were going through school and going into work unable to read or with poor reading skills. Tommy's visionary paper was well received, but trying to find ten years of funding for a high-risk, untried approach proved very difficult. With initial funding found, it was possible to start the process, with early successes leading to a wider take-up of Tommy's plans.

'I've worked as a psychologist all my life, so I've got a general background in these things. I remember saying to one head teacher in an earlier project that there are thousands of people that know a great deal about literacy and have very strong views on it. I didn't know anything about it, but I had very strong views on it, and my main view about it was that illiteracy could be fixed. My view was that the children didn't value literacy, they came from homes where literacy wasn't valued, so their attitudes, values, their whole cultural context was inimical to developing literacy skills.'

The project began not by teaching reading skills but by working to change attitudes towards reading. At the end of a pilot period, the project showed significant advances in measured literacy skills, even without any tuition in literacy.

These early results were impressive, but Tommy's aims were far more ambitious. 'What I wanted was intergenerational change that would last a lifetime and beyond. I wanted to set up something that was from the cradle to the grave and to stay around for the length of time it would allow me to be caught out if it wasn't working. That's how the West Dunbartonshire Literacy Initiative came about.'

Ten years on, Tommy's remarkable idea appears to have worked. 'Thanks to the hard work of everyone involved things have moved on considerably, and we'll be ready in two or three months to publish the final-phase report. This will show that essentially illiteracy has been eradicated, because we've now assessed all the school leavers, and we've moved from having over 20 per cent functional illiteracy amongst school leavers in 1996 to . . . well, we're down to the last three now who haven't attained the targets.'

Behind these statistics is story after story of individuals whose achievements, confidence and aspirations have been transformed as a result of their improved literacy. Tommy's ten-year report includes the perspective of one successful participant, Kathleen. 'When all this started I couldn't read, I was a failure. Now I have a cupboard full of books at home; my favourite authors are Roald Dahl and J.K. Rowling. Now I am a success.'

In keeping with Tommy's belief that lasting success would require a culture change in the whole community, the impact of the scheme can also be found amongst its many volunteers. 'One person that had a very marked impact on the project was a school lollipop lady, the woman whose job it was to patrol the crossing for the children going to school. She became one of the volunteers and was doing the intensive intervention, so we would see her out patrolling the crossing in the mornings and then later on we would see her in the school doing the intensive remedial work. That's had a significant impact on her, and she went on to work fully within the classroom after that as a classroom assistant.'

While Tommy's own drive and steadfast determination has clearly been at the heart of the initiative's success, I wanted to understand just what it was in his approach that allowed him to achieve what so many educationalists before him had been unable to achieve. He explained the thinking behind the project and the importance of what he calls 'content variables' and 'context variables'. '"Content variables" is what everybody does; it's what you put in by way of the nuts and bolts. That's how you change the curriculum: you actually do the things that will help children to learn to read. The other side is the side that is usually not looked at in interventions, and that's what I've called the "context variables". What do you need if you want to achieve something visionary, what do you need to do other than just putting in all the right content? My view was that, first of all, to do something extraordinary you need vision, but it can't just be the vision of a researcher, it needs to be a group decision. So the idea was that everybody was to be a visionary: the leader of the council, the council members, the director of education and his staff, the head teachers, the teachers at ground level, the nursery head teachers and their staff. Everybody who was going to be involved with it had to see it as being visionary and had to seek to promote their own vision of it.'

But, as Tommy was aware, vision alone is not enough, and many bold ambitions have proved unsustainable if not underpinned by an achievable delivery approach. So, alongside this focus on the visionary and the extraordinary, Tommy set out to construct an approach that was practical and affordable to deliver, and indeed to replicate. 'I've got a very strong view that you can't do this by the normal methods, which is group interventions with learning support. You have to do it by individual, intensive intervention: one person sitting in front of one child. Economically that can't be done if you've got 20 per cent of your population turning out to be reading failures. We reduced it through good early intervention to the point where numbers who were failing were small enough that we could tackle those who needed intensive individual intervention. We've trained hundreds of teachers, classroom assistants, volunteers, parents, grandmothers to carry out the intensive intervention scheme, and that's the way that we pick up the reading failures.'

Tommy is rigorous in his application of scientific method and measurement but was eager to explain that at the core of the scheme is a clearly articulated set of values. 'I've often put forward the belief that you can't separate values from science, and that the agenda of science should be driven by values. In other words, the priorities of where you put the funding, what areas you do research in, isn't a value-free decision. I've often backed it up with a quote from a social worker by the name of Bril, who said, "We believe that every single human being is of equal and infinite value. This remains true however strange, unpleasant or socially unacceptable that human being may be. It is true of helpless babyhood, lunacy and senility. It is true of the grossly subnormal, as of the highly intelligent. It is as true of the tramp as of the managing director." That is very much a kind of governing philosophy of our values.'

Tommy MacKay has achieved something quite remarkable. The learning from this visionary project will be shared and replicated across the country, ensuring that hundreds of young lives will not be constrained by poor literacy, but that all the riches of learning are opened up for them. Tommy is a visionary because he was able to revolutionise an education system to the benefit of thousands of people. But he is an inspiration because his achievements stand for something even bigger than this – the belief that, where we seek to do good, to restore justice, to create hope, nothing is ever impossible. In his words, 'We simply said when you face impossible barriers, you just need to say how do you overcome the impossibilities.'

CONCLUSION

THE BRITAIN I BELIEVE IN

' S tories,' wrote Ben Okri, are the 'secret reservoir of values'. I believe that in our national conversations we could devote more time and space to stories such as those I have told in this book. 'Change the stories individuals and nations live by and tell themselves,' says Okri and we 'change the individuals and the nations . . . if they tell themselves stories that are lies they will suffer the future consequences of those lies. If they tell themselves stories that face their own truths they will free their histories for future flowering.'

These are stories about the Britain I believe in: the real Britain of the carer, the volunteer, the responsible employer, the recycler, the ethical consumer, the charitable giver, the campaigner, the mentor. The estimated twenty million people in Britain who regularly volunteer, plus the millions more who give of their time, without ever even thinking of themselves as volunteers. The mothers and fathers helping with the local football team, lending a hand at their school, running sports days, helping with Comic Relief fundraising, joining the local campaigns to reduce waste or recycle or improve the pavements and neighbourhood. The young people running activities for their peers, mentoring younger pupils, collecting toys or clothes for children who need them more. The one in three young people who wore the white wristband of Make Poverty History. The 88 per cent of British employees who believe it is important that the organisation they work for is committed to living its values. The 81 per cent of people who gave to the Indian Ocean Tsunami appeal.

Some of these activities may be new to our times, but they are rooted in the timeless values of the good society. And it is in these millions of quiet, often uncelebrated, deeds of kindness and acts of humanity enacted every day and all over our country that we can see the greatness of Britain. It is a Britain where people recognise that it takes the willing commitment of the whole community to build a society in which individual contributions are valued and developed and potential is fulfilled. So it is a Britain where individuals can and should rise as far as their talents can take them and where the talents of each of us then contribute to the well-being and security of all: a society where we all feel a part of, and play a part in, something bigger than ourselves.

I believe there is in Britain a yearning for stronger communities, and what I have seen reinforces my belief in the capacity of individuals working together to transform communities and to change lives: a capacity that government can support and should encourage and celebrate.

'We know where the problems are,' said Richard Davis from Merseyside, 'and it's very often not difficult to come up with the solutions. Just do it. Not, "Let's form another quality circle or focus group or committee." We know where the kids are hanging out. We know there's a problem in a certain part of town; well, go and do something.'

'My life is my argument,' said Albert Schweitzer. How true that is for Richard, and for Stevie Siegerson, Avila Kilmurray, Peter Morson and others in this collection: each demonstrating every day how wrong it has been to call a neighbourhood a problem area and then give up on it, and how important it is that local people are involved and engaged. And demonstrating how important it is that government listens and then asks itself not just what is wrong but what we can learn and how might we prosper together.

Until now, our approaches have veered between relying on state action and relying on the incentives of the marketplace. Twentieth-century politics was defined by the struggle and tension between the two. Our new century calls for a new age of community and civic action: an age in which the role of government is to serve people, to empower, to encourage, to bring people together, to be partners with those working for good, and to celebrate their achievements. But this age of community has to be also an age of engagement: with our culture and communities energised and improved by the choices and actions of individuals – people power.

So it is right to recognise, celebrate and enhance the space that exists beyond the market and beyond the state: the space in which people-to-people relationships, personal choices, individual and community action can play their part – the space where voluntary and community action can flourish. It is through the willing commitment of individuals that so much support is delivered – not just from parent to child and often in later life from child to parent but also frequently from one to another bound not by familial ties but by our shared humanity. It is a culture in which we can all both give and receive across and throughout our lives.

No one put this better than Robert Kennedy, who reminded us that it is ' . . . from numberless diverse acts of courage and belief that human history is shaped. Each time a man stands up for an ideal, or acts to improve the lot of others, or strikes out against injustice, he sends forth a tiny ripple of hope, and crossing each other from a million different centres of energy and daring, those ripples build a current which can sweep down the mightiest walls of oppression and resistance.'

And the same truth applies to all the great challenges facing the world this century. Terrorism, the environment, global economic restructuring and the yearning for community: they all share one common feature. Each of them cannot be fully met without the engagement of people themselves. They cannot be fully solved by action on high, by pulling the levers, by issuing commands, or just by a wider range of incentives. Environmental advance cannot come without individuals taking responsibility and changing their everyday behaviour. Security cannot be delivered without winning the battle of hearts and minds so that moderation can be supported, tolerance promoted and extremism marginalised. Global competition cannot be met without people actively choosing to upgrade their skills. And communities cannot be built without individuals, families and groups engaging in shared endeavours.

So individuals, communities and government will have to work together in a new partnership. Ours cannot be a return to an age of the passive citizen and the all-powerful state. Nor can we return to a Victorian age in which the call for greater personal responsibility, good in itself, becomes a pretext for government to shirk its own. The partnership we seek is one where each of us plays our part: a partnership in which government does not walk by on the other side or misuse the goodwill of the voluntary sector by seeing it as a cut-price alternative but recognises what can be achieved by individuals and communities working together, and works to empower and enable people to play their full part in shaping the world in which they live. It is a partnership in which each of us – individuals, voluntary organisations and government – takes greater responsibility for building the kind of society to which we all aspire.

In government, I am committed to do more to support and empower, as well as to celebrate, all those working for the good society, because the good society depends not just on a small number of exceptional people doing extraordinary things occasionally, but on all of us doing ordinary things thoughtfully day after day: from volunteering to ethical purchasing, from supporting our neighbours to reducing and recycling.

Anthea Hare's family life and her professional training gave her the knowledge and the will to develop Richard House

Children's Hospice. Witnessing a shooting gave Erinma Bell the insight and motivation to bring communities together, collectively rejecting gun and gang violence and memorably stressing 'our streets, our communities, our problems'. It is Anne Glover's efforts to involve local residents in the regeneration of her estate that have been key to its success. And it is Jill Pay's experience and devotion as a carer that have inspired her campaigns for changes in policy. Government can't replicate that depth of understanding, but we can listen and we can learn and we can help more to do more.

It is clear that we must do even more to move beyond the old, dull and all-too-familiar 'one size fits all' solutions. Lalita Patel established her organisation not because there was no provision for elders but because existing services didn't meet local needs. Vic Ecclestone's ability to tap into the potential of the children on his estate is derived from forty years of living on the edge of the estate. Susan Langford is guiding Magic Me to break new ground because intergenerational relationships in east London are today also intercultural relationships. Projects such as these emerge from the ground up and are rooted in local needs and designed to fit local conditions. So any statutory programmes we develop must learn from this and respect the local, embrace differences, nurture initiative and encourage flexibility and choice.

This can be challenging, because government, having to account for all public money spent, is usually more cautious than the independent operator, but I have heard what Colin Zetie, Tommy MacKay, Kate King and Tom Steinberg have each said about risk. Richard Davis, working within a statutory service, was most revealing: 'Dare to fail, that's the thing. I think we should celebrate innovation. Support it. Have public services operating in a climate that supports innovation as opposed to a climate of fear.' I am committed to encouraging a stronger culture of innovation within our public services and to finding new ways of enabling individuals, families and communities to participate in actually shaping the ideas, the debates and the decisions that affect our country. And one of the ways we can continue to do this is in our support for community service for the young: from Project Scotland to the organisation V, which, launched by the then Third Sector Minister Ed Miliband and run independently and by young people, is now engaging thousands of young people in community projects from caring for the elderly to the environment.

I fully recognise that some services are best delivered by the third sector and that others, pioneered in the third sector, may be usefully adopted by government in areas where government has a duty to act. Tom Steinberg's mySociety, Avila Kilmurray's experiences in Northern Ireland, and Jacqui Nasuh's work on domestic violence all show that public services can, as they historically have, draw upon independent innovations and build from them. And I firmly believe that the future of our public services lies not in a sterile struggle for territory or a demarcation battle between public, private and voluntary provision but in the free exchange of ideas and open cooperation between the sectors. I am committed to seeking a greater role for volunteers, community groups and voluntary organisations, and to encouraging constructive collaboration in not just the delivery but, where it is the best option, the design and running of services that meet social need.

Round the country, I saw the explosion of social enterprise, and I detect a new willingness in the corporate sector for businesses to do more. Of course, businesses which are concerned about these matters in 2007 must also be seen to be concerned. Today, the transparently ethical conduct of business is as much a business imperative and a reputational issue as it is a social one. I have been inspired by a new generation of socially responsible business people such as Tom Savage, Michelle Clothier and Sam Conniff, and I believe that companies in Britain are among the global leaders in social responsibility. But there is always more to be done and more companies to involve. I commit to working with the private sector and to helping foster new thinking on how commerce and enterprise can support the creation of a more just society and the achievement of social goals.

Back in 2004, I shared with voluntary-sector leaders at the NCVO conference my belief in the independence of the voluntary sector. It was, I said then, 'the essence of their existence' and the reason why they can make a difference where others cannot. This is a belief that has been reinforced by my conversations over recent months. I have seen, and want to further strengthen, a national and local voluntary sector that, at its best, speaks to government with a confidence and legitimacy derived from its independence and first-hand experience.

In many of my conversations, I have been brought face to face with the realisation that good intentions can sometimes create unintended results and still leave gaps to be filled. Mandy Jetter and Paul Hurley offer assistance to refugees who have been dispersed across the country. Emmaus in Cambridge has grown a new model for supporting those who have fallen through the safety net. Colin Zetie of Groundwork develops tailored programmes for those who struggle to engage in mainstream unemployment schemes offered by the government. Here too government can be humble and learn, and then do more to support those on the front line.

I heard a particular plea to remember the value of small sums for small-scale projects, and as a result announced in the recent budget the new £80 million small-grants fund to meet this need. But we have to do more, and it is now a policy priority to examine how a new Social Investment Bank might help to ensure that voluntary-sector and community organisations can access more secure and sustainable funding.

Repeatedly I was reminded of the importance of the one-to-one. Dave Green's remarkable fifty-year devotion to coaching will have changed more lives than he could modestly recall.

Helen Atkins at the Poppy Project is a powerful example of what can be achieved by trust and personal support, and, as Tommy MacKay has shown, such work is not, as some critics suggest, necessarily small scale. From a starting point at which 20 per cent of the West Dunbartonshire school-leaving population were unable to read to a decent standard, he is able to report this is down to just three individuals. The success of this dedicated work, one-to-one, one by one, will not only enhance individual lives but will impact on the local economy and on the wider society for years to come. It is an inspiring but not isolated example of a man planting a tree under whose shade he does not expect to sit. I am a great enthusiast for such coaching and mentoring, and I pledge my support to the development and expansion of these and other forms of one-to-one work.

Again and again I heard about the importance of early intervention and how this approach not only gets the best results but is also the most cost-effective. Patrick Friel's experience of how the law centre enabled him to stay in training and avoid eviction and homelessness was particularly illuminating, and I was similarly struck by the determination of both Jacqui Nasuh and Benita Refson to act quickly. And I fully understand that it would, as Sharon Berry said, 'be money well spent if we could invest more in trying to maintain family ties and stop children developing mental-health problems and ending up in care themselves, making this an endless cycle'.

And I share Erinma Bell's belief that 'If we can step back and diagnose the problem and look at all the different things that are surrounding the young person, we could actually do a lot of very good preventative work before they end up in the criminal justice system. By the time they are there, it is too late. We need to be doing things before they get involved.' Our investment in Children's Centres and in Sure Start is an example of our recognition that this kind of early intervention is always the best intervention. Family support programmes, some based on the Dundee pilots that I have written about, are founded on this idea. But there are more ways we can act earlier, and I commit to the development of policies based on this imperative to act and act early.

I hope the stories in this book focus attention on the willing commitment of the British people and tell the stories that best represent – in Ben Okri's phrases – our 'own truths' and our 'secret reservoir of values'.

This book is about thirty-three people, what they have done and all that I have learnt from them and their work. But it is also about more than them. *Britain's Everyday Heroes* is about us all: what we are and what we can become. All over Britain, men and women like these arc sustaining and renewing our communities, mentoring and supporting one-to-one, and pioneering new forms of social action. They, for me, are the true celebrities and those most worthy of celebration in 2007. They have seen a need and are meeting it, often taking the path less trod and yet continuing to follow it and then breaking new ground and showing the way to us all. I admire their work, respect their achievements and pledge to support them and others like them wherever I can.

community links

NEXT STEPS

If you have been inspired by the stories in this book and want to get involved yourself, here are some signposts to organisations mentioned in this book or connected with the projects whose stories are told. Many other organisations would be keen to put the willing commitment of volunteers to good use: check with your local library to see what's going on in your area.

Interested in volunteering?

- Contact your local volunteer centre
  www.volunteering.org.uk

- Register with TimeBank
  www.timebank.org.uk

- Find opportunities to volunteer on this national database
  www.do-it.org.uk

- Check the BBC Action Network
  www.bbc.co.uk/actionnetwork

- Community Service Volunteers
  www.csv.org.uk

Interested in setting up your own group?

- Contact your local voluntary sector support agency
  www.navca.org.uk

- Visit the Volresource website
  www.volresource.org.uk

- Contact the National Council for Voluntary Organisations www.ncvo-vol.org.uk

- Publications and training from Directory of Social Change www.dsc.org.uk

Interested in mentoring or one-to-one support?

- Visit the horsesmouth website www.horsesmouth.co.uk

- Contact the Mentoring and Befriending Foundation www.mandbf.org.uk

- Chance UK mentoring for children aged 5–11 www.chanceuk.com

You don't have to join an organisation to get active: We Are What We Do is a new movement inspiring individuals to use their everyday actions to change the world.

- Visit www.wearewhatwedo.org

Organisations represented in the book

Blue Ventures
52 Avenue Road
London
N6 5DR
t: 020 8341 9819
w: www.blueventures.org

Braunstone Community Association
Forest Business Park
Oswin Road
Braunstone
Leicester
LE3 1HR
t: 0870 170 6940
e: bca@braunstone.com
w: www.braunstone.com

Bristol City Council
Arts Events and Festivals Team
Colston 33
Colston Avenue
Bristol
BS1 4UA
t: 0117 922 3719
e: arts.development@bristol.gov.uk
w: www.bristol.gov.uk

Bromley Asian Carers Association
c/o United Reformed Church
20 Widmore Road
Bromley
BR1 1RY

Community Alliance for Renewal,
Inner South Manchester Area (CARISMA)
The Saltshaker
16 Bedwell Close
Moss Side
Manchester
M16 7LN
t: 0161 227 9776
e: info@carisma.me.uk
w: www.carisma.me.uk

Chrysalis Project
t: 07780 948890 or
t: 0151 254 2640
e: friends@projectchrysalis.org.uk
w: www.projectchrysalis.org.uk

Columba 1400
Staffin
Isle of Skye
IV51 9JY
t: 01478 611400
e: info@columba1400.com
w: www.columba1400.com

The Comfrey Project
391 West Road
Newcastle upon Tyne
NE15 7PY
t: 0191 274 5588
e: comfreyproject@hotmail.com

The Community Foundation for Northern Ireland
Community House
Citylink Business Park
Albert Street
Belfast
BT12 4HQ
t: 028 9024 5927
e: info@communityfoundationni.org
w: www.communityfoundationni.org

The Dreamscheme Network
Burlington House
10–11 Ribblesdale Place
Preston
Lancs
PR1 3NA
t: 01772 251110
e: info@dreamscheme.org.uk
w: www.dreamscheme.org.uk

Emmaus Cambridge
Green End
Landbeach
Cambridge
CB25 9FD
t: 01223 863657
w: www.emmauscambridge.org

Fairtrade Foundation
Room 204, 16 Baldwin's Gardens
London
EC1N 7RJ
t: 020 7405 5942
e: mail@fairtrade.org.uk
w: www.fairtrade.org.uk

Football Unites, Racism Divides
The Stables Connexions Centre
Sharrow Lane
Sheffield
S11 8AE
t: 0114 255 3156
e: enquiries@furd.org
w: www.furd.org

Groundwork East London
6 Lower Clapton Road
Hackney
London
E5 OPD
t: 020 8985 1755
e: contact@groundworkeastlondon.org
w: www.groundwork-eastlondon.org.uk

Livity
Tunstall Studios
34–44 Tunstall Road
London
SW9 8DA
t: 020 7326 5979
e: livity@livity.co.uk
w: www.livity.co.uk

Magic Me
18 Victoria Park Square
London
E2 9PF
t: 020 3222 6064
e: info@magicme.co.uk
w: www.magicme.co.uk

Merseyside Fire and Rescue
Youth Engagement Team
46 Derby Road
Kirkdale
Liverpool
t: 0151 296 5250
w: www.merseyfire.gov.uk

mySociety.org
12 Duke's Road
London
WC1H 9AD
e: team@mysociety.org
w: www.mysociety.org

NCH Dundee Families Project
Dundee Intensive Support Project
57 Blackcroft
Dundee
DD4 6AT
t: 01382 455709

Newham and Essex Beagles
Newham Leisure Centre
281 Prince Regent Lane
London
E13 8SD
t: 020 7511 4477
w: www.neb2005.co.uk

The Place2Be
Wapping Telephone Exchange
Royal Mint Street
London
E1 8LQ
t: 020 7780 6189
e: enquiries@theplace2be.org.uk
w: www.theplace2be.org.uk

The Poppy Project
Eaves Housing
2nd Floor Lincoln House
1–3 Brixton Road
London
SW9 6DE
t: 020 7840 7141
w: www.eaves4women.co.uk

Richard House Children's Hospice
Richard House Drive
London
E16 3RG
t: 020 7511 0222
w: www.richardhouse.org.uk

Storybook Dads
HM Prison Dartmoor
Princetown
Yelverton
Devon
PL20 6RR
e: storybookdads@blueyonder.co.uk
w: www.storybookdads.org.uk

Streetwise Community Law Centre
1–3 Anerley Station Road
London
SE20 8PY
t: 020 8778 5854

Streetwise Opera
26 Binney Street
London
W1K 5BN
t: 020 7495 3133
e: admin@streetwiseopera.org
w: www.streetwiseopera.org

Time Together
c/o TimeBank
2nd Floor Downstream Building
1 London Bridge
London
SE1 9BG
t: 020 7785 6363
e: mentor@timebank.org.uk
w: www.timetogether.org.uk

COMMUNITY LINKS

Community Links is an innovative inner-city charity running community-based projects in east London. Founded in 1977, Community Links supports over 50,000 vulnerable children, young people and adults every year, coping daily with the consequences of poverty and struggling with the causes. Not just financial hardship, but poverty of experience and – perhaps most crushing – poverty of expectation. The organisation is a catalyst for change and brings together support from business leaders, volunteers, funders, government and service users to tackle some of the country's most intractable problems and, in learning from that process, shares knowledge and experience from the ground up.

As well as first-class service delivery for the local population, Community Links is a pioneer in creating new ways of collaborating. Early demonstrations of partnership between charities and business from the City and Canary Wharf have set a model for others to follow. Rigorous analysis of local conditions and the public-service innovations needed to improve them have resulted in changes in national policy.

Community Links is also the birthplace of We Are What We Do, the new international movement that inspires people to use their everyday actions to change the world. For these and for many other examples of restless innovation, I am delighted to offer the proceeds from this book to Community Links to support the continuation of their inspirational work.

Community Links
105 Barking Road
Canning Town
London
E16 4HQ
020 7473 2270
www.community-links.org